Wakefield Press

PLACES
WOMEN
MAKE

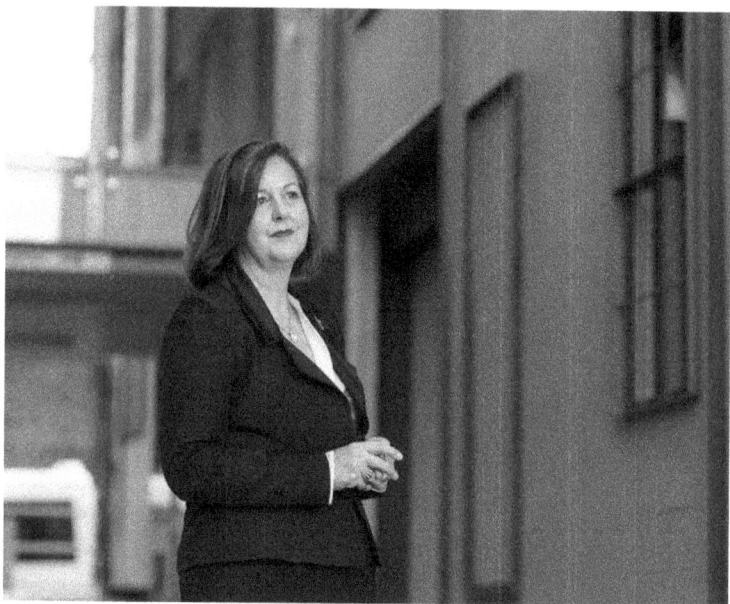

JANE JOSE *is an urbanist, author and CEO of Sydney Community Foundation. Cities and community life are her passion. In this book she celebrates women who have given us places that are loved and suggests how essential this contribution will be to making cities more liveable for future generations.*

PLACES WOMEN MAKE

Unearthing the contribution of women to our cities

JANE JOSE

Wakefield
Press

Wakefield Press
16 Rose Street
Mile End
South Australia 5031
www.wakefieldpress.com.au

First published 2016
Reprinted with revisions 2016

Cover designed by Liz Nicholson, designBITE
Text designed and typeset by Wakefield Press
Printed in Australia by Griffin Digital, Adelaide

National Library of Australia Cataloguing-in-Publication entry

Creator: Jose, Jane, author.
Title: Places women make: unearthing the contribution of women to
                our cities / Jane Jose.
ISBN: 978 1 74305 394 2 (paperback).
Subjects: Women and city planning – Australia.
                Urban women – Australia – Social conditions.
                Women – Australia – Attitudes.
                Community development, Urban.
                Social participation – Australia.
Dewey Number: 305.40994

CORIOLE
McLAREN VALE

For my sons with love
. . . and for tomorrow's children

CONTENTS

Designing a dream city is easy,
rebuilding a living one takes imagination.

THE DEATH AND LIFE OF GREAT AMERICAN CITIES, 1961,
JANE JACOBS, HUMANIST AND URBANIST

PREFACE

Australia is one of the world's most urbanised countries, with eighty-nine per cent of its population living in urban areas primarily on the eastern seaboard. Yet the written and visual narratives about women that I grew up with were about women in the outback. As a farmer's daughter I did not question that. I lived in isolated areas, where women created homes and community places against the odds. The stories of the Drover's Wife, Daisy Bates and Ruby Langford were the stories that captured our imagination. I can think of no urban heroine from my youth.

Jane Jose redresses this imbalance as she explores and records the contribution women make to improving the liveability of our urban places. She sees women as the unsung heroines of our cities. What a pleasure it is to read the stories of women who have become major players in shaping our cities. And women married to powerful men who were not afraid to use their influence to improve the public domain when power was not available to them. I asked myself why I had I not heard of Diamantina Roma, the wife of Brisbane's first Governor, Sir George Ferguson Bowen, who in 1859 arrived in Brisbane. Brisbane will never be the same to me as I walk through Roma Street and recall the words of the then Governor-General, Quentin Bryce:

> I think of her influence in the salons of Brisbane, meeting people in its dusty streets, encouraging music and culture, establishing hospital facilities, motivating her peers and charming foreign and local visitors.

There are many other women we meet in this book whose names will be unfamiliar to readers, despite their contributions as activists, architects, writers, landscape architects, local government leaders and philanthropists.

There is sympathy and understanding for those women architects and designers who worked with their partners and received little recognition for their work. There can be no better illustration of this than the architects and designers of Canberra, Walter Burley Griffin and his wife Marion Mahony Griffin. It was years before the scope of Marion Mahony's work was understood, although there is no evidence that she felt undervalued. However, when the woman in the partnership is invisible, the loss is not just personal. It has unintended consequences and suggests that there is a lack of female competency, interest and capacity in the design of our urban spaces. The evidence suggests otherwise, as the rise of young women architects, engineers and designers form social media groups and lobby for a stronger role in their environment.

Women are passionately interested in the design of their urban spaces.

Jane Jose has invited us into her life as an urbanist, a title she assumed as she increasingly worked in the world of planners and architects. She cares deeply about urban spaces and has spent much of her professional life trying to make them better places for communities to flourish. The book is warm, engaging and optimistic, and encourages us to celebrate our newly discovered urban heroines.

Jane Jose has written *Places Women Make* at exactly the right time. The city of the future is now our living room and the generation born in the 1980s is likely to be Australia's first apartment-dwelling generation. It will look to shared public places for its sense of belonging to a community. As women's participation in the workforce rises and families move to the inner city, we will live differently. We need the skills and sensibility of women to create special places, places where the architecture is not hostile to the spaces women make.

Any woman who wants to change her world can start by picking up this book and be inspired to action by the number of women upon whose shoulders she can stand.

Wendy McCarthy, AO
Feminist, Educator, Community Leader

INTRODUCTION

THE CITY IS OUR
LIVING ROOM

Up amongst the treetops of the old figs that circle the driveway of Number 8 Birtley Place, Elizabeth Bay, I first became an apartment dweller. This mansard-roofed, textured brick building is a local landmark in Sydney's east. A flat in one of Australia's first high-rise apartment buildings, designed in 1934 by the architect Emil Sodersten, was my first real experience of urban life. It was Sydney, but inside the building with its art deco flourish, it felt like Manhattan.

Before that, like many baby boomer Australians, I had lived in a house that had a garden. For me it was in a quiet street in Adelaide. Elizabeth Bay and Potts Point, where I now live, is Sydney's mini Manhattan, not so quiet, yet maybe Australia's ideal urban village. Moving from a house and garden to live without my own backyard meant that the city, its street cafés and parks, and especially its harbourside parks, quickly became my outdoor living room, a retreat on Sunday morning with a book or the papers. I learned that the way public places are designed and what they offer us changes our mood and how we feel as we live every day. And more and more Australians – and indeed global citizens – will be living in apartments in the twenty-first century. Shared public places and the way they are created will be crucial to successful, enjoyable urban life.

Places Women Make tells stories of the nurturing places that women have given us. It is about the kinds of places women have made in our cities that make them better places to be. It is about how people can live with a greater sense of belonging in cities. Women are the uncelebrated urban heroines of our cities. They have done much to make Australia's cities and communities better places to live in; however, their stories are not as visible as those of the men who mostly design the buildings in our cities. Cities are man-made places, and mostly the work of men, but there are places shaped by women. The stories told here have been remembered and gathered over more than twenty years of working with communities and with leading women city-makers and they recognise the enormous contribution of women to making Australian cities more beautiful, lively and full of delight. *Places Women Make* shows there is a body of urban work by women who have made places happen in Australian cities. My investigations on the influence of women on our cities revealed that in many of the places I have visited and fallen in love with, women had been responsible for making them.

In Australia men have been the hero architects of most of Australia's city buildings, leading the design, even if women were invisibly designing the detail behind the scenes. The stories in this book celebrate the places in cities we know women have given us, places that nurture, surprise or cocoon. I have chosen places that provide delight and enjoyment; I am not proving a theory about the skills of men versus those of women, but simply suggesting that women need to be more involved in the future shaping of our cities, as we can all benefit from the sensibilities that women bring to the planning process. When we look back at the inspired decisions and magnificent places created by women in this country, it is clear we need feminine sensibility to solve the challenges of life in a more urban world. We need more contributions from women, and certainly their creativity, their intuition and their often lateral approach.

We know a female perspective is different from that of a man. It is needed more than ever in the complexity of contemporary urban life. Women from all walks of life have used their gifts, their courage, their imagination and their generosity to create places to make the lives of others better; they have used their creativity and ingenuity to claim abandoned places to improve, change, preserve or reuse. They have given us places that enrich us, lift our spirits, teach us, excite and surprise us and sometimes just make life a little bit more beautiful.

Making change and building anything in cities is a slow process, often difficult, sometimes tedious, and almost always fraught with community politics. Some of the most exciting places in cities are accidental, but most are made. They touch generations beyond the time of those who inspired them and created them, and they influence other cities and communities to grow and change.

Cities are the playrooms of our lives, holding our past and promising our future. As we crowd into cities to live and work and as jobs force us to become more mobile, our cities are becoming shared places, places in which we stay and spend time when we are not at home and not at work. People are increasingly aware of how cities can make them feel and choose one over another because of what it offers. The generation born in the 1980s, who urbanists call 'the millennials', are likely to be Australia's first apartment-dwelling generation, having opted to live closer to work and choosing the sense of belonging, convenience and connection of an urban rather than a suburban lifestyle. Those who leave the city for a town by the sea or in the mountains or for a house in a smaller city will still want good places to share village life, places where they can connect and make communities. And now with more mobility and with more people living alone, belonging to a community becomes even more important to a meaningful life.

Although cities have grown hugely over the past one hundred years, people remain villagers at heart. Children growing up in apartments still need trees to climb. We need to see the green of a garden and the blue sky above.

The city is now our living room. We want the 'house and garden' comfort and style of home in our local streets and parks and in the shared places of the city. At weekends we go out for coffee, to galleries and libraries, or just to walk and hang out with strangers in charming, lively public places that enable us to feel alive, stimulated and aware that we belong to a shared humanity. We don't live in one house for our entire adult life anymore. At each stage of our life, and as we live longer, we redefine our needs and where we want to be.

Places Women Make is mostly concerned with Australia's major cities and the Australian women who have contributed to shaping them. For each of the women and places about which I write there are many other untold stories. I hear new stories every day in my work in communities. Many of the women have achieved their work with the help of supportive men; they have stood behind capable women, as women have stood, less visibly, for centuries behind the success of men.

Listening and talking is the way women love to work. It is both instinctive and quickly learned. Women are natural storytellers and homemakers. These are essential skills for working with communities to construct places that meet other people's needs. Today, in communities across cities everywhere there are sisterhoods of women working together to build successful neighbourhoods, cities and communities.

For more than two thousand years, since the Greeks designed the public square and the Plaka, men have been the architects of our cities; yet women have worked in complex, often indirect, ways to make the places we need. Now women make things happen as catalysts, advocates, activists, commissioning clients, donors, influencers, philanthropists, decision-makers, architects and urban planners; but it is still rare for women to be the hero architects of public buildings and places.

Many of the women decision-makers involved in shaping cities tell the same story. They begin as activists, agitating for change, often at their own kitchen table and then take up the cause of creating better places in their neighbourhoods and cities. Some of the most exciting initiatives have occurred when communities, often led by female campaigners, have demanded more from governments and developers. The US urbanist and activist, Jane Jacobs, guardian of Manhattan's Greenwich Village in the 1960s and 1970s, can still be a role model to young people today. Jane Jacobs changed the way a whole generation of planners, architects, civic leaders and activists thought about the shaping of our cities. The human qualities she argued for in cities are just as relevant to the young millennials today, who will be shaping the way they live. Jane Jacobs was fearless in her advocacy and unafraid to speak out against car dominance, freeways and the loss of local heritage, arguing for human-scale buildings and healthy cities. Now the neighbourhood she saved, Manhattan's Greenwich Village, is on the way to the High Line, the ultimate outdoor living room. The High Line is a place she would have loved. The baby boomer generation grew up with the protest songs of that time and a generation of women listened to the sweet voices of Joan Baez, Joni Mitchell and Mary Travers, encouraging us to believe we could change the world, defeat racism and sexism, and save the environment, heritage and nature from the excesses of modernity. Most of these challenges are still with us, as are the songs. And women continue to be strong voices in calls for change and for more room for women in every sphere of urban, community and professional life.

Why *Places Women Make?* Why write about women and cities when mostly men are the architects of our city buildings? Almost all of the major accolades for city-making in history and in contemporary awards systems, such as the Pritzker Prize for Architecture and the Nobel Prize, have been awarded to men. Female architects who have won major awards for public places and buildings are still too rare. As one leading woman architect I interviewed explained to me: 'since the Greeks created the Plaka as a gathering place where women were not allowed and since the Romans created civic life, men have led as the architects of our cities all over the world'.

Having worked in the mostly male-led world of city-making for the past twenty years, I am convinced that our cities would be different if more women were involved in shaping them for tomorrow's children. As more women graduate from architecture, engineering, design and planning, perhaps cities can change to become more nurturing, friendly and humanist? Will communities gain from more women leading the design of places? Would our cities be different or more welcoming if women had played a larger role in their design? These are questions explored in *Places Women Make*.

Research into the contribution made by women to Australia's cities uncovers a plethora of hidden stories. The walks and parks, private gardens, music bowls, museums, secret gardens, libraries and sea pools described in these stories carry the warmth and spirit of the women who inspired them.

As a young woman I was drawn into the politics of city-making to help transform inner-city Adelaide into a better place for its people and to preserve its colonial heritage. Adelaide is a city of one million, the capital of South Australia, and where I grew up and had a family. There are all kinds of ways to become involved in making our neighbourhoods and cities connected, more delightful, surprising and beautiful. Community leadership is just one.

Melbourne, where I was born, with its focus on redesigning the inner city and reinventing its heritage, inspired me as a young civic leader. Adelaide led me to act to preserve aspects of the city I valued – to keep its sense of history and of being a big country town under a desert sky, although still a city. Community service led me to Canberra, first to serve on boards, and later to work with government and the community on changes to government urban policy to ensure a more urban, less suburban and more sustainable future. Sydney is home now and, as Australia's global city, it has all the challenges of a fast-growing metropolis. These are the cities I know well and so I share the stories of what women have given them, and to Australia's other major cities.

In the book *City Limits* by the team who led Australia's leading think tank on cities, the Grattan Institute, Jane-Francis Kelly describes Australia's cities as broken, although she argues that they can be fixed. They may not all be broken, but many places in our cities and neighbourhoods have never been cared for. Governments won't make the cities and places we want: we have to shape them ourselves, first into places and then into communities. And then they shape us.

By sharing stories about women and the places they have made in our cities, I hope to inspire a new generation of women to imagine and create the kinds of places that will be loved and enjoyed by tomorrow's children. For cities are the playrooms of our lives, holding our past and promising our future.

Still admired, young **ELIZABETH MACQUARIE**'*s influence on contemporary Sydney has enriched city life.*

A
WOMAN'S
PLACE

Civic leader and humanist, **CLOVER MOORE**,
who made the villages of inner Sydney places for everyone.

SAFE HANDS

As you grow older you discover that you have two hands,
one for helping yourself and the other for helping others.

AUDREY HEPBURN

A s soon as we step out of the door, the city landscape is everything we see and experience. It is as complex as any ecosystem. Architects have not always designed places that make us feel alive and comfortable when we are in shared places. Could women do this better? We don't know, since our cities have been almost completely designed by men.

What we do know is that a woman's place is no longer only in the home. We know too that city-making and achieving what is desirable for your town or suburb are complex activities and hard work. We know that when cities work for women they work for everybody. We pass on magnificent places from one generation to the next, but places change and community needs change, and each generation must be part of the process of making the places in which they will live.

The work of creating cities is always concerned with balance: what to add, what to keep and what to change. It takes moral courage to hold onto *and* to add the kinds of places we need for our time and for those who follow. Women leaders have demonstrated they can be trustworthy custodians of our cities – a pair of safe hands.

Making wholesale change in cities can be a fraught and difficult process, while developing new places, parks and buildings can be slow. Changing some parts of our cities and, therefore, community life may take two decades. Designing change in the city is a skilful job, one that requires sensitivity, imagination, courage and intelligence. It is a long tough process, involving more than design and funding, but also political and community acceptance. Australia's cities are blessed with natural beauty, rivers, mountains, harbours and heritage, and these add to the quality of our life. However, it is the places we make ourselves that allow us to enjoy city life in fulfilling and engaging ways and which add to a place's beauty and attractiveness. The best of these places arise from their communities, not from governments. We need to guide governments, hold them to account and call for what we want.

In Sydney there are places that have endured and which have been loved by generations. Mrs Macquarie's Road is a walk that remains a hugely popular destination. First created in the early 1800s for the afternoon walk of Governor Lachlan Macquarie's wife, Elizabeth, it was a place to stroll in the cooling sea breezes. Still snaking around the glorious shaded edge of the harbour, it has become for people living in city apartments in the twenty-first century an exercise track or a beautiful path into the city; it is also a popular tourist mecca. Cities are enriched by places of enduring beauty and interest. The best cities can be walked, and have parks and paths where we can meander and experience a little connection to nature, even if it's just blue sky and birdsong.

The High Line in New York is a contemporary model for an old idea, a place for the locals to wander and encounter friends, a place people can identify with. The designers have created a patch of wild planting – nature in the city! The High Line developed from a community idea of reusing an abandoned rail track high above the traffic of Manhattan. It made the transition from an idea to a project with the support of powerful women in New York – Chief City Planner Amanda Burden and Democrat City Councillor Christine Quinn, with early funding from fashion designer Diane von Furstenberg. It has become a model for other cities, as more and more people want places to walk, enjoy the sunshine and meet friends.

Sydney has the Goods Line, its own version of the High Line: a connection from the Central Station to Darling Harbour as a new walking connection. The late Robyn Kemmis, a former Deputy Lord Mayor of Sydney, is given credit for the idea of this brilliant walkway and for being determined to see it delivered, as it was by landscape architect Sacha Coles and the team of talented young women in Sacha's studio. The Sydney Goods Line has creative spaces and places for pop-up cafés, galleries and bars. A generation of millennial entrepreneurs using social media can create a marketplace anywhere. In a world where so many connections take place online we need attractive, safe, shared public places in our cities and towns to enable 'real' – face-to-face – connections that build belonging.

People want places to delight and surprise and calm them in the streets, squares, parks, and footpaths. They love public art and even when particular pieces are disliked, it causes community argument and is something shared to talk about.

Landscape architecture as a profession began in America in the nineteenth and early twentieth centuries and women were immediately drawn to it. Women as landscape architects began to claim the places between the buildings for their designs – as the men focused on being the architects of the great buildings. In cities, the places between the buildings are often more important because they are the places everyone uses. It was not until the 1950s however that landscape architecture acquired professional status in Australia and now many more women practise as landscape architects here than as architects. The records of the Australian Institute of Landscape Architects estimate that about forty per cent of the practising profession are women. Perhaps the holistic 'house and garden' approach of urban design still attracts women.

In Australia, Melbourne's Edna Walling was known as a gardener rather than a landscape architect, but she was certainly a designer. Her art was to blend house and garden, to work to shape the whole in tune with the sense of place. She is a leader in the movement of women in Australia choosing landscape architecture as a way to shape the city and how it is used. More of Edna Walling's story later.

In the late nineteenth century, society accepted this extension of the gentle art of drawing and gardening – landscape architecture – as suitable work for the women who were drawn to architecture; the power play of the creation of the metropolis was claimed by men. In America the story of women architects is quite different from that of Australia and Britain. By the early twentieth century in America women were enrolled in architecture, with large numbers in Chicago and San Francisco particularly. Their male counterparts went off to Harvard or to the École des Beaux-Arts in Paris!

America has long celebrated the work of famous women architects: Julia Morgan, one of the best known of women architects in the US, designed William Randolph Hearst's fantasy castle on the hills outside San Francisco. This elaborate castle–home, with its dreamlike confusion of styles, including part of a Roman temple, took more than a decade to build. In her book about Julia Morgan, *Architect of Dreams*, Ginger Wadsworth writes:

> Julia turned 35 in 1907. At that time, only a handful of women were architects and they had to work full time to succeed in a career dominated by men. If Julia dreamed of marriage and children, she never talked about it.

She has no peer in Australian cities. Julia Morgan left a large body of work: in her forty-seven-year career she was commissioned to design seven hundred structures, including many great twentieth-century buildings in San Francisco, at Berkeley and in the national parks.

It was to be another American architect, Marion Mahony Griffin, who would become Australia's most celebrated woman architect and role model, but not in her lifetime. Australia's most prestigious award for a woman's contribution to architecture carries her name.

Architectural scholars agree now that Canberra is the one city in Australia that has been drawn by the hand of a woman. We can only speculate that Canberra would be an even more beautiful city had

Marion Mahony's drawings been more closely followed. Her story and her pivotal part in the Burley Griffin design for Canberra comes later.

For now, a return to that nagging question: does it matter that so few women have designed city buildings in Australian cities? Is there a difference between the designs, sensibility and approach of men and women as designers? Why have so few women been the architects of our cities and public places? Why have so few been recognised for the places whose creation they have assisted? Why has city-making not been entrusted to women or been seized by them?

A number of women have been vocal and visible campaigners in the public life of cities but rarely as architects. Many more women architects have worked as generous, giving and unseen partners, wives, muses, assistants and volunteers. Our cities are full of plaques and nineteenth-century statues commemorating the efforts, leadership, achievements and good works of men in Australian society. There are few statues celebrating women from the era of European settlement in Australian cities, apart from the queens of England. The achievements of ordinary women were not celebrated in this way until the feminist movement of the 1970s, when busts began to appear in public places, like those of the poet Judith Wright, who sits in Canberra's Civic centre, and the suffragette Mary Lee on Adelaide's North Terrace. Sydney's inner-city parks are scattered with statues of celebrated men – Governor Phillip, Captain Cook, Lachlan Macquarie, William Daley and even Robert Bruce. Queen Victoria is an exception, aloft on a pedestal outside the magnificent Victorian shopping arcade, the Queen Victoria Building. Where is Marion Mahony, as a prominent acknowledgement of her role as co-designer of Australia's national capital?

While social patterns are changing, in Australia women remain the primary nurturers, care givers, mothers and grandmothers as part of the cycle of life, nature and nurture. They know how small simple changes like shady trees, paths, seats in a street and parks where children can play and dogs run make daily life better for everyone. Their nurturing instinct has much to offer in the design of public places in a more urban community.

In Australia women are still often challenged when they set out to promote change. Women who have been successful leaders and made a difference in a city claim that their capacity to make change was questioned when they began the task of shaping a place in the city. Leaders like the Irish humanitarian Mary Robinson and Sydney Lord Mayor Clover Moore acknowledge that for most women their political campaigns begin around the kitchen table, with a belief that 'they can do it'. Both women say they have often been warned that they're likely to fail. Being told they won't be able to achieve something often acts as the impetus that drives courageous women forward. At a forum run by the climate change activist group, 1 Million Women, Mary Robinson spoke of movements that began at the kitchen table. 1 Million Women, funded by Sydney philanthropist Tara Hunt and founded by Natalie Isaacs at her kitchen table in Sydney's Northern Beaches, adopts a practical focus in a global movement, encouraging women to cut back on carbon emissions and showing them simple ways to share ideas to save energy and reduce emissions. This local community leadership is an example of women wanting to use the power of women in daily life to lead a global movement for change.

Clover Moore has proved to be a safe pair of hands for Sydney. Like many women who begin as opponents to poor-quality development, she moved on from protest to action and has overseen the creation of wonderful places. Clover Moore began with a passion about a local community issue close to where she lived: she wanted a patch of grass for her children to play on rather than the knee-grazing, green-painted concrete of the local park. The former Adelaide Lord Mayor and politician, Jane Lomax Smith, wanted to stop a multi-storey hotel being built in her neighbourhood street of original colonial nineteenth-century cottages and row houses and went on to be a civic leader – for the next twenty years. One of the first women to hold the role of Lord Mayor of Melbourne, Winsome McCaughey, began her time in Melbourne's civic life as an activist, plotting at her kitchen table. On one Sunday afternoon, with fifty neighbours gathered at her inner-city villa, she planned a community movement to protect the grand heritage streetscape of Melbourne's elegant boulevard, Collins Street, and the laneways of the inner city. She has much to be thanked for. The work of transforming Melbourne's inner-city laneways to living rooms continues, with the human-scale buildings, the warehouses and laneways continually being reinvented by each generation's creative stamp. Perth's Lord Mayor Lisa Scaffidi used the profits of the last mining boom to invest city funds in public spaces, making Perth a more enjoyable, attractive city with community and civic meeting places at its heart. Anna Bligh, as Arts Minister for Queensland and later as Premier, backed the expansion of Brisbane's cultural life by creating new places at Southbank, making it a thriving inner-city arts precinct. So many of the stories of the change effected by the hands of women share the same storylines – women with moral courage and determination succeeding in civic roles as city-makers in what was traditionally a man's world.

City-making is not only about making new places and buildings; it is as much about preserving good places and their connection to what surrounds them, adapting them sensitively for new times. It is about communities discovering new ways of living. Beginning with Marion Mahony Griffin, who drew the gardened boulevard city of Canberra and imagined a lake at its heart, creative women have led urban movements in many places and in many ways, unafraid to change the way we use cities, bringing new experiences and richer choices to their communities, from bike riding and community gardens, to local markets and public art. Small-scale places matter as much as the grand in scale and can be vast in their importance to the sense of community and their generosity to strangers.

American urbanist Jane Jacobs famously said big plans could lead to mistakes. 'Big plans never stirred women's blood. Women have always been willing to consider little plans.'

ETERNITY

Hope is the thing with feathers
That perches in the soul
And sings the tune without the words
And never stops at all.

EMILY DICKINSON

Clover Moore is a courageous reformer. For decades, through a period of great social change, her influence on community life in Sydney has been immense and significant. She stands apart from other political figures in Australia in her early support for equal rights for the gay community in Sydney and beyond, and in her early belief in and action for the real challenge of climate change.

The inner-city villages of Sydney where her constituents live have blossomed under her watch. New street markets, community gardens, street furniture, pop-ups, pocket parks and pools, all with a local character that comes from the people who live there, have built a sense of connection and belonging to places that were once just ordinary inner-suburban streets. Clover Moore takes the long view. She has given hope and made small changes to places that add up to big improvements in people's everyday lives. I worked with her to shape the village plans built around Sydney's main streets, translating the ideas from her community. She listened and delivered. In local government the stakes are high and the personal rewards for tireless work are low. The reward is the satisfaction of seeing places and communities blossom over time, as public places are improved.

Under Clover Moore's guiding hands Sydney's revitalised public places have transformed the inner-city area. Dozens of small redesigned public squares and parks have been recognised with awards for their excellence in community engagement, architecture, urban design and planning. The conversion of Sydney's main street since settlement, George Street, to a pedestrian street with a tram is an idea that Clover Moore led with persistence until the state government, through Minister Gladys Berejiklian's support, finally agreed. Clover Moore describes her approach as focusing on direct representation rather than being driven by a particular ideology. 'I defend our public estate and take on the vested interests.'

The women who have shaped our cities have been brave and have often had to struggle against the prevailing current. As we have seen, the influence of women in city life in Australia has rarely been as the architect. The roles of influencer, catalyst, leader, advocate, activist, and decision-maker are not easy. When the drive to develop cities is motivated by profit and ignores the needs of people, the legal battle lines are often drawn.

Architects who are aware of community needs work with sensitivity with developers to design not only the building but also to improve the surrounding places.

In Australia now almost equal numbers of young men and women graduate in architecture. Parlour: women, equity, architecture, an activist group of Australian women architects, has brought the issues of gender equity to the surface. A Parlour research project, led by Professor Naomi Stead at the University of Queensland, with active support from the architectural writer and design advocate Justine Clark, and taken on as a vital policy issue by Melbourne architect Shelley Penn when she was National President of the profession's peak body, has led to the implementation of equity guidelines for architecture. The aim is to promote change and foster a culture in architecture studios where more women are designers and registered architects. In 2013 when Parlour began, only twenty per cent of women graduates became registered architects. Registration enables architects to design and build places in our cities and towns. Parlour has highlighted the need for more women to reach the top of the profession and to lead at the design table. It has had a degree of success in some policy change, but the glass ceiling has barely been penetrated. Most of Australia's female architects work on houses, with only a very small, albeit increasing, number working on the design of public places; even fewer lead as designer. In the virtual world of online chat, women architect networks discuss the poor treatment of women in architecture studios in the US, Britain and Canada, calling for more equality in pay and opportunity.

Outside the closely knit family of architects across the world, very few people can name celebrated women architects. A few Australians and Americans might name the contemporary practitioner, Zaha Hadid, or Marion Mahony Griffin, for her involvement in the design of the national capital. Marion Mahony Griffin is perhaps the most unrecognised heroine of city-making anywhere. As the wife of Walter Burley Griffin, she worked with him, drawing the designs that won the competition for Australia's national capital, Canberra. No one quite knows how substantial her influence in the design of Canberra was; yet, Walter acknowledged her drawing work when he won the competition, which he entered in his name only. Perhaps he maintained this position of single authorship, because in Australia at the time it was not seen as appropriate for women of her social position to work, let alone influence the design of a city. Having worked first in the studio of the great American architect, Frank Lloyd Wright, and as one of the first women to graduate as an architect in America, Marion Mahony Griffin is believed to have designed far more for both Lloyd Wright and Burley Griffin than was ever acknowledged.

The Iraqi-British architect, Dame Zaha Hadid, winner of some of the world's leading architectural prizes, including the Pritzker Prize, is one of only a handful of women alongside the men who are the 'starchitects' of modern urban life. In 2000 years of civilisation and cities this is a short list.

An obituary in the *London Financial Times* for Scottish architect Kathryn Findlay, who died in 2013, written by the architect Edwin Heathcote reflects on the paucity of opportunities for women architects in Britain in the twentieth century. He notes: 'Miss Hadid herself built nothing in Britain for decades'. He commends the design talent of Findlay: 'it is now more common to see successful women architects than it was twenty years ago. Findlay and her generation cleared the ground. But it was tough going'.

While it continues to be rare for women to win commissions to design and build major buildings, more and more women are achieving success in elections for civic, political and community leaders and are serving on governing authorities and driving cultural agendas and change. Across Australia local government has had many effective women administrators leading councils. Monica Barone, working alongside Lord Mayor Clover Moore, has delivered improvements to inner-city Sydney and its villages. Before her, Katie Lahey was Chief Executive to Lord Mayor Frank Sartor and Lucy Turnbull followed him as the first female Lord Mayor of Sydney. Jude Munro in Brisbane is recognised for her hand in the inner-city transformation of Brisbane to a more cosmopolitan city and before that she worked alongside Lord Mayor Jane Lomax Smith in Adelaide, delivering a long-term plan for Adelaide's Park Lands and cultural boulevard, North Terrace.

Few women in Australia have chosen the role of the imaginative 'heroine' architect, speaking up for the needs of citizens and designing public places in our cities. Rachel Neeson, winner of a Sulman Award for Public Architecture in Sydney, is a role model in her work with landscape architect Sue Barnsley. They are a female team who win public projects in the city, such as a new entrance to the Australian Museum.

A number of women architects are prominent and effective commentators, notably Associate Professor Elizabeth Farrelly, Professor Dimity Reed and Shelley Penn. Elizabeth began as a critic of architecture but has broadened her perspective to become a commentator on cities and city life. She argues that women's thinking should be at least equal if not dominant in place making. Speaking on a panel at the Sydney Opera House's 'All About Women' series, she says: 'we need women to be equally involved in the biggest issue of our time – saving the planet. We need the wisdom of women to help get this done'. The way we manage our cities will be key to this challenge.

There is a growing number of women online chattering on global websites, such as Women in Architecture, discussing gender issues. In the next generation of rising women architects, this will surely change, with the voices of more women architects leading public debate on how our cities should be shaped.

Women take a long view, acting as intergenerational custodians for their children, tomorrow's children, and they care what happens to strangers. There is a pattern of strong women in civic life who have been unafraid to question proposed development or to call for more for their communities than they are being offered. Women questioning the merits of development are not always opposing development: they are often seeking to have input into shaping change or calling for what Sydney Lord Mayor Clover Moore describes as 'sensitive design'. Clover Moore will be applauded by future generations for returning inner Sydney to a great tree-lined city of connected urban villages, with places to walk and cycle and paths by which to reach its spectacular harbourside parks.

Cities are layered and absorb the spirit of the people who make the places within them. The architects and designers, the artists and landscape architects, the shopkeepers and café owners stamp our streets and communities with their imagination. These places need the female spirit as well as the male. The stories of the places I love, whose stories are told here, include libraries, parks, gardens, walks, museums and galleries, places for concerts, heritage buildings, good streets, community gardens and sea pools. All have emerged through the persistence, imagination and drive of women.

Looking back helps us to look forward intelligently. Using social media, women architects worldwide are discussing the possibilities for their colleagues who want to play an equal role in city-making in the twenty-first century. The various elements of our lives and lifestyles change as we move through the different phases of life. Growing up in a house with a garden, then moving into a flat, returning to a house and garden to bring up children and moving as an empty-nester into an inner-city apartment, I know it is essential to be able to escape to enjoy nature in a nearby park. Parks are vital urban lifelines. In every stage of life we can enjoy the great public places of cities; indeed, I have never needed them more than now, as an apartment dweller without a garden living in a city of four million people.

Sydney is a city blessed by its geography, with inlets and waterfronts, rivers and sea to its north, south, east and west. People who live, like me, in an inner-city village of Sydney – Potts Point, Glebe, Woolloomooloo, Pyrmont, McMahons Point, Kirribilli, Newtown and others – celebrate the harbour-edge walks, parks and secret gardens which enrich our urban lives. Each year, as more people move into cities across Australia and Asia, many more beautiful and calm green places will need to be created in cities, places where people can experience nature and perhaps even hear birdsong under the blue sky.

In a few decades of working with and talking and listening to people from communities across Australia, I have learned that some of the best places to be in are those made with passion, hope, love and community involvement, very often influenced or led by women.

As the wife of an early Brisbane Governor,
CONTESSA DIAMENTINA ROMA BOWEN *was an influence*
in civilising the city, supporting the arts and care for those in need.

A CIVILISING INFLUENCE

We shall win more by being soft, so I am going to be
wise as a serpent and harmless as a dove.

MAYBANKE ANDERSON

Sydney has much of Australia's finest colonial architecture, and a woman used her influence to ensure that it was built. In 1809 Elizabeth Henrietta Macquarie travelled from Scotland to Sydney. This was a brave journey for a young woman from a known world to an unknown one. Mrs Macquarie was to influence forever the township of the small but thriving British penal colony of New South Wales, which was to become the great city of Sydney.

Young Elizabeth Macquarie arrived aged thirty-four, in her prime, in a privileged position as the wife of Governor Lachlan Macquarie. She was a woman without power but with influence. Using all her female strength, she urged for the establishment of standards to ensure great architecture and a European culture, for Sydney to be designed with public gardens and walks, and for women and children to be cared for in ways that would help to civilise the convict settlement.

The entry on Elizabeth Macquarie by Marjorie Barnard in the *Australian Dictionary of Biography* tells us 'she took a kindly interest in the welfare of women convicts and of the aboriginals' and she is described as 'intelligently interested in gardening and architecture'. Other historic records describe her as sketcher, landscape gardener, architectural designer, patron, diarist and philanthropist. She was an early patron of the arts, even commissioning artists, including

John Lewin, whose wonderful painting of fish is a favourite of mine in the Art Gallery of South Australia's colonial room. Joseph Lycett, a convict artist, was her landscape painter and the architectural draughtsman who implemented her ideas. In his folio views he described Mrs Macquarie's Walk as:

> an excellent promenade, more than three miles and a half in circumference . . . laid out under the direction of Mrs. Macquarie . . . whose fine taste has been wonderfully displayed and very generally admired in various parts of the Colony, but more particularly at the Government House and gardens at Parramatta.

Her books on architecture brought by her from England became resources for the convict who became Government Architect, Francis Greenway.

Sydney was a wild place when Elizabeth Macquarie arrived from Airds in the Scottish Highlands in 1810. She may have been prepared for the wild natural landscape by the stark beauty and space of the Scottish landscape where she grew up, but nothing could really have prepared her for the convict society of Sydney. Convicts, prostitution, rum, drunkenness, extremes of climate, the unexpected landscape, the Indigenous inhabitants and the animals and insects never before been seen by Europeans were awaiting Elizabeth Macquarie. The city was a place where people could get ahead in any way possible – and little has changed in more than two hundred years; Sydney's door is open and it remains a place of opportunity if people have something to offer. Today, many Europeans visiting Sydney for the first time still regard a trip 'down under' as an adventure into an unpredictable place.

Mrs Macquarie must have loved the smell of the bush and the sea and the strange sounds of bird life on the quiet harbour headlands of the settlement. Her favourite place and the one for which she is most remembered is Mrs Macquarie's Road. The road, cut into the hill by convict labour, was through bush and led to a seat carved especially for her. Mrs Macquarie's chair is carved from stone to resemble the throne from the legend of Arthur and Guinevere. From her chair at the point she could survey the picturesque landscape falling to the harbour's edge, look across the water to the tiny white coves of beach and watch the tall ships sail in. Little has changed in the scene as she saw it. Her walk still circles the edge of the headland and many of Sydney's great gathering places. Without Mrs Macquarie's adventurous spirit the walk may never have been built. She urged Lachlan Macquarie to create great public places in the convict township. She took a long view and with Lachlan created the Royal Botanic Gardens and the Domain at the city's edge. I feel the sense of history and an attachment to Elizabeth Macquarie every time I walk along the busy path or cross through the Domain to Macquarie Street – still Sydney's most elegant street.

Knowing that she walked the harbourside path and that perhaps Barangaroo, the wife of the Aboriginal elder, Bennelong, who lived on nearby Goat Island in Sydney Harbour when the British colonists arrived, walked it too makes it a special place. Today, Elizabeth Macquarie's story – her love and adoption of this place and the path she walked – has ensured that the walk survived for future generations, linking the past to the present. Nearby is Sydney's Domain. It is a great green park surrounded by old grand and gnarled fig trees. It has become Sydney's outdoor performance space, a place where the Sydney Festival's First Night happens, when the streets and parks and squares are filled with performances and the city truly becomes the people's living room. The Domain is still a place where people share the joy of free concerts under the stars: Opera in the Park, Carols by Candlelight and Symphony in the Park. It is a place to gather for celebration or in grief. Just after I arrived in Sydney I walked from Elizabeth Bay across to the Domain to join thousands in a communal grieving for the loss of young people in the 2002 Bali bombing. Generally the Domain is a place for joyful gathering but, importantly, it is a place the city community claims as its own, for celebration or grieving.

Along the roadway built by the convicts for Elizabeth Macquarie's afternoon walk are two of Australia's great public places, the Art Gallery of New South Wales and the Royal Botanic Gardens. The gardens are on land Mrs Macquarie enjoyed before it was transformed into the public garden it is today. When walking through the gardens it is still possible to see the first street trees ever planted in Australia. Perhaps the addition of street trees to Sydney is another of the influences of Elizabeth Macquarie. The garden's information reads:

> This row of Swamp Mahoganies, *eucalyptus robusta*, is the oldest known street tree planting in Australia. The trees were planted here about 1816 along the original route of Mrs. Macquarie's Road.

These places remain great public places in Sydney and add to the quality of life for everyone. Walks, shady trees and gardens in cities are important these days when so many people live in apartments, with a balcony at best. Visitors to Sydney, city workers and locals wanting to spend time in a cool and calm space make the trip to these great public places of the inner city. For those who don't have a garden at home, these shared places are a lifeline to nature, with all its calm beauty. Elizabeth Macquarie might be surprised to know how many people still clamber up to the stone chair carved for her pleasure more than two hundred years ago. On any day it is a scene of Chinese, American and European visitors sitting on the great seat and taking pictures to email off or tweet out to a world beyond Sydney.

Written on the face of the rock at Mrs Macquarie's Chair are these words:

> Be it thus recorded that the road
> Round the inside of the Government Domain called
> Mrs. Macquarie's Road
> So named by the Governor on account of her having originally planned it
> Measuring 3 miles and 377 yards
> Was finally completed on the 13th day of June 1816.

Elizabeth Macquarie's influence endures. The simple rustic sandstone bridges she walked are still to be seen in the Royal Botanic Gardens when we come across them by chance, and the elegant Regency architecture of the Macquarie Lighthouse at North Head reflects the high standard for public architecture she established in Australia. The Female Orphans School in Sydney's west at Parramatta, a building still in public use as part of the University of Western Sydney, was modelled on Mrs Macquarie's family home in Airds. Today it is celebrated as a great example of early Australian Georgian architecture and is a reflection of Elizabeth Macquarie's refined eye for design. It demonstrates that well-designed buildings and places last, even if, or perhaps because, their use may change. Together Elizabeth and Lachlan Macquarie began the work of making the small convict colony of Sydney town into a civilised city. They ruled with kindness, spending just over ten years in Sydney, although they departed dismayed by the corruption of the governing officers.

Elizabeth Macquarie was not an openly strident campaigner, but her letters in the Mitchell Library reveal that she was politically astute and opinionated, had courage and common sense and exerted a strong influence on her husband. In the book *In Her Own Words: The writings of Elizabeth Macquarie*, the author Robin Walsh says:

> As the woman behind 'the father of Australia' a term she coined on his gravestone on the Isle of Mull, Scotland; power gave her the freedom to tart up the Sydney landscape at her whim. Government Houses at Sydney, Parramatta et al. were richly beautified.

She took the only path open to women of her position at the time, to influence the direction and the decisions of the man in power. But she took a long view. Like many women she used her role of significant other to good purpose. Young, bright, adventurous and idealistic, she had the courage to shape the city and the society in which she lived, at a time when women's choices were limited. By looking back at what women in the past have given our cities, we can see the value of their long view, their civilising influence, and the interest in community that women of influence gave to Australian cities in their infancy.

In colonial Australia, women were unable to work or marry the freed convicts who were beginning to shape the young nation and they were at risk. Caroline Chisholm helped women to achieve both, and later advocated for land to be made available to enable settlers to establish small farms. Through the Family Colonization Loan Society founded by her in London, she assisted more than three thousand people to travel to Australia, also advocating for better shipboard conditions for the courageous women who travelled across the sea. Her character, as history reveals it, accords with that of many of the women whose stories I tell. She is described in historic records 'as determined in a feminine way'. Today we might call her a social philanthropist.

Lady Franklin, wife of the colonial governor of Van Diemen's Land, Sir John Franklin, is described in Alison Alexander's book *The Ambitions of Jane Franklin: Victorian Lady Explorer* as 'running a petticoat government in Van Diemen's Land'. Lady Franklin, in common with many pioneering colonist women, supported the work of her husband in the ways that the society of the time would accept and allow. Her influence on the cultural life in Tasmania resonates today in Hobart's recent reinvention as a cultural tourism destination. More of her adventurous story comes later.

Another of the wives who brought a civilising influence to a colonial town was Diamantina Roma, the wife of Brisbane's first Governor, Sir George Ferguson Bowen, who in 1859 arrived in Brisbane, the city in which she would live as the leading lady of her times. In a speech given by Australia's first woman to be appointed to the most powerful role in the country, that of Governor-General of Australia and representative of the Queen of Australia, Queenslander Quentin Bryce reflects on the influence of Diamantina Roma.

We should recall her influence in the salons of Brisbane, meeting people in its dusty streets, encouraging music and culture, establishing hospital facilities, motivating her peers and charming foreign and local visitors.

In colonial Australia these women of status, the wives of powerful men, had influence on the issues and protocols in the new colonial society. Like Elizabeth Macquarie, who had left the rugged landscape of Scotland, Diamantina Roma had left behind her childhood home on one of the Ionian Islands between Greece and Venice. She is described in historic records as: 'a beautiful Greek fairy princess'. She is remembered today by the places that were named after her – Roma Street, the Roma Street Station and Diamantina River.

Other women who arrived in less privileged circumstances embraced their new home far from civilised Europe, creating and building as they saw necessary. Mary Reiby founded Australia's first bank, lending money from her simple cottage. Her bank became the Bank of New South Wales, now Westpac. The site of her small house – Mary Reiby Place – is located near Sydney's Circular Quay. Hers could well be the title of founding mother of Sydney as the global financial centre it is today.

The places whose development was influenced by these women and the changes in attitudes to women that these women effected – from gaining equity, to the need for work, to overcoming homelessness and advocating for democratic rights – are still an inspiration today as women continue to strive to reach an equal place in all endeavours of Australian life alongside men. Young mobile women with global careers making their lives in different cities far from where they spent their childhood can still use their imagination to find ways to contribute to their new communities.

Australia's colonial women and wives recognised what was needed to make the new society cultured and habitable, and became involved in shaping their society, as well as, in some instances, the lives of others. Educated women were not restricted to domestic affairs. They were a resource, supporting their husband's work, while remaining careful not to disrupt the convention that women should be confined to the role of homemaker and hostess. Bright capable women must have found these challenging times. Married working-class women were treated more as equals, taken seriously and found authority in running the household.

Women such as Elizabeth Macquarie and Caroline Chisholm, and later the leaders of the early Australian suffragette movement, who fought for votes and rights for women, did this in the ways that were available to them at the time. By writing and sharing new ideas amongst themselves and other women, they could set the agendas for the men who were the politicians of the day. Adelaide's Catherine Helen Spence and later Mary Lee, Melbourne's Vida Goldstein, Sydney's Maybanke Anderson and Louisa Lawson, Brisbane's Emma Miller, Tasmania's Jessie Spinks Rooke, despite the differences in the times in which they lived, their situations and their class, were kindred spirits. Through writing and publishing, they created a national movement aimed at improving the lives of the women and children in their communities. This desire to make an impact, to change attitudes or to make an idea a reality propelled them.

Today's young women rightly seek power, not merely influence, and for mobile twenty-first-century women there is no better way to become part of the community than to become involved in community life. Pat Hall, a community worker in Warwick Farm, in western Sydney, is supported by the Sydney Women's Fund, a group of philanthropic professional women who support women and children in Sydney; she is fundraising and actively campaigning to get a basketball court for one of Australia's most disadvantaged suburbs. Times change and needs change, but women still answer the call to campaign for the places their community needs. City life needs activists. Making welcoming spaces calls for women with courage, power, influence, knowledge and skill to shape the change they seek.

Many women from the past and the present are extraordinary and inspiring role models. For every story included here there are dozens of untold stories from women in all walks of life who notice what their communities need and they act – sometimes loudly, sometimes invisibly – to make it happen.

Living in Potts Point in Sydney means that I often walk along Mrs Macquarie's Road on my way into the city. When I do, I invariably experience a sense of gratitude for an inheritance from people who had the imagination to dream that a great city with great public places could be built here. When I think about Elizabeth Macquarie I am reminded of how beautiful Sydney Harbour, with its still trees and bush and jagged coves and inlets, must have been over two hundred years ago. Her seat must have been a serene and remarkable place from which she could look out across the bay and see only the sea, sky and bush, as the tall ships sailed in towards Circular Quay. Elizabeth Macquarie's influence shaped a city. The harbour's other bush-covered headlands concealed naval forts and were places women would fight for more than a hundred years later to preserve as bush. When I sit in her seat now in the evening light, the bay looks serene and calm and I find it hard to imagine that the great global city of Sydney is pumping away just around the cove. These historic places have influenced present-day Sydney profoundly and make the city's centre the remarkable place it is. A place I have come to love.

COMMITMENT AND
COMMON SENSE

People always told me you'll never do that . . .

CLOVER MOORE

The public spectacle that is Sydney Harbour is overwhelmingly beautiful. The rough cut of the sandstone cliffs, the wild angophora, the scrappy eucalypts with branches waving like unruly arms, the old European gardens falling to the water's edge, the sheer jagged rock, little sandy coves, glimpses of aqua-blue water and mighty headlands; all this has changed very little since settlement. The shoreline places remain for people to explore, and they hint at Australia's untamable inland. Mrs Macquarie's path is still enticing and can be approached from one of the oldest parts of the city. Start from Elizabeth Bay House, now a house museum and once home to Alexander Macleay, one of Sydney's founding colonists. It overlooks part of the original garden and the deep blue of the harbour stretching across to North Head. From there it is a short, steep walk up stairs to Macleay Street and down Challis Avenue, past the all-day café scene.

Pass the grand terraces of local Potts Point residents, including former Australian Prime Minister Paul Keating's perfectly restored Victorian terrace. Descend the hundred-plus steep stairs at the end of Challis Avenue from Potts Point towards the wharves of Woolloomooloo, where the scene changes from café to defence. Naval ships are often parked at the gates of the misnamed Garden Island. It is neither a garden nor an island but an active naval base of the Australian Navy, a high-security spot in the heart of the city. Named by convicts who tried to grow food there, Garden Island was established to protect Sydney Harbour from invasion. These days it occasionally welcomes an invasion of tourists, who pour out of the super cruise ships that arrive like great floating hotels.

Walking down past the Garden Island gate you reach Harry's Café de Wheels, with its aroma of grease, sizzle and sausage attracting fossicking seagulls, the odd water rat and other hungry mouths. Walk along Cowper Bay Road, ugly and uneventful until the grand turquoise-and-white Woolloomooloo wharf buildings. Saved from demolition in the 1970s as part of the 'green ban' preservation movement that spared so much of early Sydney and its bushy headlands. The wharves, which date from 1897, have been converted into a hip international hotel, the choice of rock stars, bands and cool corporate visitors. It's hard to imagine the rationale behind the proposal for the demolition of these extraordinary industrial wharves, with their great gantries. The place now hums with activity, with a boardwalk and lively restaurant life, while a few lucky millionaires live in apartments at the harbour end.

The wharves were saved in the environmental protests spearheaded by women, which led to the imposition of green bans, with the help of the trade unionist, Jack Mundey, and the militant Builders Labourers Federation, who supported the housewife activists. The cultural activist, Elsa Atkins, who led the National Trust in New South Wales for many years, says women were key to this protest.

The enduring value of heritage places is sometimes conveniently overlooked when short-term profits suggest their replacement! Yet, both the great wharves of Woolloomooloo and Walsh Bay have been reinvented to be exciting new places in the city. They still have their old soul, but now theatre and festival patrons, café and restaurant crowds and a few well-heeled residents can enjoy the layers of the past with the energy of Sydney's cultural riches.

Among the Sydney women who led the forceful wave of opposition that saved some of Sydney's most valuable heritage places – from the

Rocks to Woolloomooloo – was the urban planner Joan Masterman. As a woman in the largely male planning, design and development world of the 1970s, she was one of a group of women who formed the Wharves Committee. The women ultimately enlisted the support of the powerful New South Wales Deputy Premier Jack Ferguson, who valued the work of the tradesmen who had built these remarkable structures and convinced the premier of the day to save them. It was a woman's way to solve the problem: to find the 'right button to press' using an intuitive approach. Sydney would be less without these old wharves.

As you walk from the Woolloomooloo wharves along the board-walk and past a row of luxury cruisers you are led to one of Sydney Harbour's many magical stairs. Climb up the worn sandstone stairs, criss-crossed with fig tree roots, and rise up to Mrs Macquarie's Road. Along past the bottlebrushes, darting birds, brightly coloured parrots and lapping water you walk. If the ghost of Mrs Macquarie still takes this walk, she must enjoy the buff young men who have claimed the Andrew (Boy) Charlton Pool as theirs. Named after a famous Aussie swimmer, Boy Charlton, it must be one of the finest lap pools in the world, an outdoor paradise, where swimmers are accompanied by shrieking cockatoos. The pool is the only twentieth-century building on Elizabeth Macquarie's Road. Outdoor sea pools are part of Sydney life and have been for centuries. Around the turn of the twentieth century, sea pools were demanded by women who wanted safe and private areas of the beach to swim with their children and away from the gaze of men; there is still a women-only sea pool in the Sydney beach suburb of Coogee.

The most beautiful sea pool of all is tucked away in a bay on the south coast at Gerringong. Sheltered by a headland, the pool stays calm while waves from the ocean beyond crash onto the sea wall. The local women from the dairy country, the landscape that Lloyd Rees later painted, wrote to the state parliament in the late 1800s, lobbying for the funds for the pool. They chose the best site and soon the men came to use the pool too. And it still gives everyone pleasure.

Mrs Macquarie's path offers a bird's-eye view of the bodies sunning themselves at the Boy Charlton pool, and then the path continues around the cove. Families, singles, couples of all shapes, ages, sizes and nationalities, bikers, skaters, babies, runners, swimmers and tourists parade along Mrs Macquarie's track past the sea walls, rocks and lapping sea. Neither the track nor the barnacle-covered rocks of the coastline has changed since earlier times. Perhaps the path traced a track already there, one walked by Barangaroo: two women from different worlds seeing the same beauty. This is a place from the past still cherished in our time.

For a city of over four million people there is a remarkable amount of bush at the heart of Sydney. Mrs Macquarie's walk tells a story of European settlement; yet, there is an earlier more ancient Aboriginal history now being told.

Under the governing hand of another woman, the Lord Mayor of Sydney, Clover Moore, artists were engaged to begin to trace Mrs Macquarie's path to tell the story of the Aboriginal Eora nation, the people on whose country the small settlement of Sydney town was first built. Their story is now part of Sydney's story as understanding grows between the first Australians and those who have come as settlers and their descendants since 1788. Eora Journey tells the story of Barangaroo and Bennelong, who lived as a couple and as leaders of their people on Goat Island, in the inner harbour.

The headland known as Mrs Macquarie's Chair is the starting point of the walk called Eora Journey, extending from Circular Quay, from there to Mrs Macquarie's Chair and on to the inner-city suburb of Redfern, a special place for Indigenous Australians. Redfern is where a former Australian Prime Minister, Paul Keating, gave the historic Redfern Address, in 1992, when he called for a new relationship of reconciliation between Aboriginal Australians and the later European arrivals.

Two hundred years from the time the Macquaries were making their grand plans for Sydney, Lord Mayor Clover Moore won the right to rule – not merely to influence – sharing a commitment and common sense inspired by Elizabeth Macquarie, and with the same passion for well-designed city building that Governor Lachlan Macquarie once gave to Sydney.

Clover Moore is the first woman to be publicly elected rather than being appointed to the traditional male role of Lord Mayor of Sydney. Despite having served the citizens of Sydney for more than two decades as a member of parliament and being elected as an independent leader in thirteen elections, many of the true conservatives in Sydney's media, business and politics have vehemently opposed her work. Politicians on both sides of mainstream political parties have challenged her vision for a more sustainable city. Supported by the people who live and work in the city, she transformed the city villages with many wonderful public places. As a leader, she encouraged people to think through the social issues of the times, including reconciliation, climate change and gay marriage. As Lord Mayor of Sydney, she pushed for a project to help reconciliation between black and white Australians and to tell the story of the Eora nation, the first people to live on the shores of Sydney Harbour.

The Eora Journey walk will have a special significance. The idea came first from the local Indigenous community as part of Sustainable Sydney 2030, an urban planning vision for the city led by Clover Moore. Conversation and engagement with communities is a trademark of Clover Moore's leadership style. In a very female way she supports listening and dialogue with people and turns to experts to provide answers and to direct her actions. In her words, her advisors possess: 'sensitivity to design and to community'.

Talking with Clover Moore in the Lord Mayor's office, I share a pot of tea warmed by a homely hand-knitted tea cozy. She will be remembered as a female community leader who provided ethical leadership through a turbulent decade of state politics, which saw five state premiers in power as she got on with the job of setting an agenda for a more sustainable inner city. We talk as women do, sharing tea and ideas. Proud of her political success, she remains modest, warm and sincere, focused on what needs to be done for the people of

Sydney. She is a private woman with a public life and comfortable and committed to leading in her own way. Elected Lord Mayor in 2004, she says:

> I didn't plan to run as Lord Mayor, it was a call from the public.
> I provided new leadership for the city and the urban environment, representing the community not party political manipulation.

Anyone who has worked closely with Clover Moore knows the pace she keeps and marvels at her freshness, energy and radiance. In spite of more than twenty years of achievements in improving public places and the lives of the disadvantaged people in the city, she is aware that her work is not finished. 'Creating great public places remains one of my highest public priorities, creating places where people want to be, to stop and linger rather than rushing through', she says. She then pauses and adds:

> my greatest contribution has been the work of developing Sustainable Sydney 2030. It is about a sustainable city. It means you can have people living in high densities but they have wonderful facilities, parks and places to go to and we are contributing to saving the planet for the future.

She tells me that as a child she used to give her father a tree for birthdays or Father's Day to add to the local bush and he would plant it and she would tend it, often replanting it herself to make sure it would thrive.

Eora Journey is one of many projects that have made Sydney a more inclusive society, with its people and visitors made more aware of Indigenous history. As a city public art project, it has been shaped by the City of Sydney's Architect, Bridget Smyth, and the Aboriginal cultural leader and art curator, Hettie Perkins, who worked with architect Julie Cracknell.

Clover Moore's public conversations with the community showed her that the people wanted Sydney to be a more humane city, a good, fair place to live. Australians have been reluctant to embrace and understand Aboriginal culture and in Sydney Aboriginal people seem sadly invisible. Perhaps the walk will recognise that Barangaroo, the wife of Australia's best-known Aboriginal man, would almost certainly have walked over the same ground as Elizabeth Macquarie, looking out to see the men returning with fish for dinner. Barangaroo has her own story, which is surfacing now. Aboriginal elders say she was a feisty and noble woman, a leader of the Gadigal people who stood equally alongside Bennelong. Bennelong, who lived from 1764 to 1813, has been immortalised in our history with the naming of Bennelong Point, the site of the Sydney Opera House. Now Barangaroo is the name given to a major new part of the city being built overlooking Goat Island, where Bennelong and Barangaroo lived. At Barangaroo, a headland park mimicking the original shoreline has been added as a harbour-front walk in the spirit of Mrs Macquarie's walk.

Barangaroo is famously said to have told the early British colonists to 'go away' but like her husband Bennelong she later sought connection to them. It is thought the couple lived in a hut built by the British where the Opera House stands today. The Indigenous academic, Associate Professor Wendy Brady, tells her story on the City of Sydney website, Barani. The website telling Sydney's Indigenous history is another innovation of Clover Moore.

Clover Moore has demonstrated a practical way of leading change in community attitudes and behaviour by involving people in making the changes that promote sharing and understanding of other cultures. From community gardens for growing healthy food, cycle paths for healthy transport and the adoption of green technologies, to developing walks that enable people to learn about their history and about the original Aboriginal ancestors and the land, her approach is to encourage people to participate.

One of Sydney's leading architects, a man who designed a number of major public places in Sydney, once criticised her to me for having paid too much attention to the small public places and parks in the city rather than driving major projects. He described the small projects she is promoting in the city as being 'like tatting'. To my mind this shows a lack of understanding of how women see the small things adding up to a greater whole. His comment ignores the change she has overseen in attitudes and how people live in the changing world of the city. An exciting, surprising, beautiful, liveable city bears the fruit of a strong economy. These are the changes that attract talented people to choose Sydney as a place to live and to make their contribution to Australian life. Clover Moore understands that community places and activities are the glue in the community, drawing people together, helping people to question and rethink ideas and even how they live their lives.

Women leaders understand that small improvements across cities, such as seats and shade in neighbourhoods and main streets, add up to a better daily life in the living room of the city for everyone, irrespective of their wealth. Working on the small things is not an alternative to major precinct schemes, but the human impact when the detail is right makes them count.

As the first woman Lord Mayor elected by the people, the popular and charismatic Clover Moore was swept into office. This followed the removal of the Sydney City Council and the redrawing of the boundaries by the NSW State Government. There was fury from the residents at the removal of the council and Lord Mayor Lucy Turnbull, who had been appointed to the role of Lord Mayor after the previous mayor, Frank Sartor, had moved to state parliament. Clover Moore was approached by her community to run for office and she won. On the three occasions she won the office of Lord Mayor she was strongly supported by the votes of the 180,000 residents living in the City of Sydney Council area surrounding the centre of Australia's largest city.

At my first meeting with Clover Moore, the force of her presence reminded me of that of a mother superior. Perhaps it was her Irish face echoing the tradition of the Celtic Christian church, where women led communities and did good deeds. Her bright and intense eyes, her wide smile, her authority, her aura of calm and the collar-like neck chokers she wore at that time reminded me of a robed nun with her calm authority. Clover Moore is known to be a devout and driven woman. She is quick-witted, with a sense of humour. She is truly passionate about her work in the community and has the certainty of purpose that accompanies this drive. She expects from those around her the same commitment she gives. With her authority and determination is a rare mix of innocence and kindness, not often seen in astute and successful politicians.

A huge crowd listened to her reflections in her valedictory speech on her last day as a member of the NSW Parliament. Legislation had been introduced to prevent her and others serving both in local and state assemblies to retain both roles. She told the story of how she had been drawn into public life as a young mother in Redfern wanting grass in the park for her children to play on. 'I was told it was easier to sweep up the broken glass from bottles on the concrete. I walked the streets pushing a pram, formed a community group, and was elected and got the grass'. Under her watch Redfern began to change and to attract a new urban generation of creative people to live and work amongst its clean pavements, grassy playgrounds, well-lit, shady tree-lined streets, cafés and shops and parks.

Clover Moore has been a courageous reformer. Her work focused on improving the villages of Sydney where her constituents live has, in the female way, taken a long view of what will be in the best interests of the community. I worked closely with the Lord Mayor and her urban design team for six years on committees and later on writing the village plans for inner Sydney as policies that she embraced and implemented. For her, the role of Lord Mayor is to represent people, rather than present an ideology. 'I defend our public estate and take on the vested interests', she bravely claims. Cities have and will always need women of courage and common sense like Elizabeth Macquarie and Clover Moore, women who take a long view.

Sustainable Sydney 2030, the plan that Clover Moore sees as her most important work, required the ethical leadership she provided. It needed her practical questioning, her courage and desire to have a conversation with the community and to dare to challenge the way things had always been done. She was one of the first Australian leaders to embrace the challenges of climate change. The cycle path network appearing across Sydney and changing how the next generation will move around the city is a consequence of her vision for her city in a changing world. The long-term plan for improvements to inner Sydney continues to unfold across the city and will make urban life more rewarding for coming generations.

Sydney, with its chaos and crowding, is an exciting city. It is a city not just for locals but it is also important for all Australians as the place where white settlement and where the Australia we know began. Melbourne was settled as Port Phillip in 1836, was planned and has an order and grandeur that Sydney has never had and never will. Sydney, a convict town settled in 1788, retains its spirit as a city that town planning cannot tame.

Women can now make a choice to be part of civic life as a people's representative or a public servant in a way that was not possible for women like Elizabeth Macquarie. The improvements in the City of Sydney that Clover Moore as Lord Mayor and CEO Monica Barone have delivered exemplify what women can achieve in roles that were once not imagined could be accomplished by women. In the old world order the Lord Mayor was a man and the administrator was the Town Clerk, a position also held by a man; the only role for women was the Lady Mayoress!

One of Clover Moore and Monica Barone's gifts to the city is the Surry Hills Community Centre and Library in inner-city Sydney. This centre is an example of new thinking and could not be more different from the traditional library, with its nineteenth-century grandeur. This is a library for the twenty-first century in every way, especially in its architectural design. Clover Moore was the driving force in the decision to provide not just a library, but also a community and childcare centre. And it would also be in a space that could demonstrate how to create a sustainable building using recycled energy and water and with a low carbon footprint. It has slotted into the main street of Surry Hills, Crown Street, and is the hub at the centre of the village wheel. This is a street that in the past two decades has been transformed. It was once a two-lane road with heavy traffic; now it is a place with wide footpaths where people wander and promenade happily. The library joins local cafés, wine bars and pubs, quirky and stylish shops and a much-loved neighbourhood park, where children play after school and people flock for the Saturday market. The library is the final piece of a jigsaw that is one of Sydney's most loved inner suburbs, attracting people from all over the city.

The Surry Hills Library and Community Centre doesn't offer quite as many activities as Bryant Park and the New York Library, where a program of events are run seven days a week, from yoga to language or dancing classes, but it comes close. The Surry Hills library's 'what's on' information promises to 'expand your world'. It offers storytelling; writers in conversation; talks on probably almost any topic imaginable; social media sessions on parenting; history and ancestry; an open concept platform; arts stations for drawing, sketching and writing; and sessions on architecture. Books are housed on the ground and basement levels, with the childcare centre on the upper level.

As women leaders, Clover Moore and Monica Barone see libraries as community hubs that give people access to all kinds of learning, information and services.

At Green Square, in inner-city Sydney, a young female competition-winning architect, Felicity Stewart, with her partner Matthias Hollenstein, from the firm Stewart Hollenstein, are shaping a new place. Their aim is to redefine the traditional idea of a library so that it reflects the dynamics of people's lives – from reading in a garden, to going to a library as a café.

Part of Clover Moore's legacy has been to provide a new kind of library. Libraries have always been important but are growing in significance to communities as we live in the age of knowledge.

Although many women still choose the female way of influencing change rather than the often brutal bear pit of politics and government administration. Having contested and won thirteen local and state government elections in a little more than twenty years, Clover Moore has been the first woman to hold office for long enough to have a major influence as a decision-maker on Sydney. Serving as an independent member of parliament, representing the inner city for twenty-four years, and in local government for fifteen years with three terms as Lord Mayor, she has been a strong hand in a velvet glove.

Courage is necessary to enter what is still a man's world of city-making. Clover Moore says her greatest inspiration is US writer Stephen Covey and his book *The 7 Habits of Highly Effective People*, with its proven principles of fairness, integrity, honesty and human dignity. It became clear when working with her that she has a moral compass to guide her through rough times. She speaks of 'huge battles to get there' in making improvements to the city:

> The public meetings where I went to talk about the improvements to Redfern Park and the new sports ground were amongst the most violent crowds I have faced. One night it took actor Russell Crowe, co-owner of Sydney football team, the Rabbitohs, to get up and say 'why are you attacking her when she is trying to improve your community?' He got a rabid, violent crowd to back off.

Australian city life is about much more than making buildings. In earlier times city-making was about taming nature and mimicking the architecture of British cities. Now it means shared community experiences and being out under the wide Australian sky, enjoying the sunshine, the wind, the shade and shelter of trees, community gardens and the parks, the libraries and the places we go when we use the city as a home away from home. The influence, creativity and leadership of women are needed if our cities are to give us the places we need, as apartment life becomes a more common choice for people as a way to live.

MARION MAHONY GRIFFIN, *the woman who designed a city.*

WOMEN DESIGNERS

RACHEL NEESON, *architect, mother and leader in her profession, designing public places; winner of the Sulman Award for Public Architecture in Sydney.*

CLAIMING THE CITY

The end, our aim, is to find a way to cure our sick civilization, to make it possible for our communities to function wholesomely, free from disease. This cannot be done unless we have a properly organized community.

MARION MAHONY GRIFFIN, *THE MAGIC OF AMERICA*, 1949

If Marion Mahony Griffin was worried about a sick civilisation a hundred years ago, what would she think now? The United Nations predicts that nine billion people may live in cities across the planet by 2050; at the time of writing fifty-four per cent of people now live in cities compared with ten per cent in 1900. In Asia each year one million people are moving from the country to the city. The Australia Institute predicts Australia will have a population of forty million by 2060.

It has become harder to create the ideal community life Marion Mahony Griffin hoped for – a 'properly organized community'. People find themselves like the rolling stones of Bob Dylan's song, we are 'on our own, a complete unknown, like a rolling stone' – strangers in new places. He could easily have been singing about the challenge of urban life in the twenty-first century. There is now the constant movement of skilled and unskilled people and young educated people, who lead mobile lives following work and resettling far from the extended tribe of family and friends, needing to find an instant sense of belonging in a different culture, city, town and community.

What might Canberra have been like if the human-scale City Beautiful movement behind Walter and Marion's plans had been more closely followed? Worldwide, there is an online movement advocating for women architects to become acknowledged for the places they have made, and the call is for them to be given more space at the design table. While it has taken a long time for her to be fully recognised, in a sense Marion Mahony Griffin has been one of the catalysts for this movement, with the celebration of the centenary of Canberra in 2013 more fully acknowledging and celebrating her work as an architect and designer.

In Australia, women architects like Rachel Neeson, Kerstin Thompson, Penny Fuller, Camilla Block, Felicity Stewart, Hannah Tribe, Emma Williamson, Penny Collins, Abbie Galvin and others are now recognised for the quality of their work. They are new role models as women working on public projects. Many women follow in the tradition of women architects – partnering with men in practice and often working as a husband-and-wife team. Wendy Lewin has worked alongside Glen Murcutt for decades. An early Australian exemplar was of course Walter Burley Griffin and Marion Mahony Griffin. It's the nature of architecture that work and life are inseparable. Huw Turner and Penny Collins, partners in life and in architecture as Collins and Turner, were awarded the prestigious Sulman Award in 2013 for designing a centre for Sydney's Waterloo community. It is a robust, gutsy building: concrete, green walls, low budget and long life. It is one of Clover Moore's projects to meet local needs.

Architects have often married architects but normally only the man has received the accolades. Women played other roles, as muse, accountant, wife–confidante and illustrator – or any combination of these – with the woman supporting the man's career. Penelope Seidler studied architecture, but it was her husband Harry who gained fame and recognition as a great Australian architect. She was his constant support. Women architects were often and still are effective partners to their architect husbands, running the office behind the scenes. It is said that but for Marion Mahony Griffin the competition entry for the design of Canberra would never have been completed, posted and there on time (*The Dream of a Century*, National Library of Australia, notes by curator Christopher Vernon). Now women architects work alone, while others are the truly equal half of husband-and-wife partnerships, such as Lindsay and Kerry Clare, who were jointly awarded a Gold Medal for their State Library of Queensland. The building at Brisbane's Southbank is already a much-loved hub for people of all ages.

There is now a worldwide movement of women architects setting up their own studios to bring women's influence to the design of public places. The contemporary American architect, Jeanne Gang, who leads Studio Gang Architecture, is a Chicago-based architect recognised as one of the leading female architects in America. She says she 'seeks to answer questions that lie locally at the heart of communities – site, culture, and people – and that resound globally – diversity, climate and sustainability'. These are universal and timeless themes.

The one area of public place design in Australia where women's hands have long been at work is in landscapes, public gardens and urban design. Women worked on the early landscape and urban design of Canberra. The British landscape architect, Dame Sylvia Crowe, is well known for her work in the national capital, but the many young women who worked alongside the men who were architects leading the design of Canberra's great public buildings and their surrounding landscapes remain unnamed and unknown.

Vita Sackville-West's much-loved garden at Sissinghurst in the Kent countryside, south of London, is from the tradition of women as landscape gardeners, creators of house and garden. The tradition began with British landscape gardener Gertrude Jekyll and was led in Australia by Melbourne's Edna Walling. It has always been seen as respectable for women to work in the garden and to create the house and garden as a whole.

In cities women have also more easily succeeded in claiming the spaces between the buildings and the places where plants grow and children play as theirs to shape, taking the holistic approach of fitting in with what is there. Until late in the twentieth century the city was another place altogether. It was a man's world. It was only from the

1970s and the feminist movement that women started working after marriage in many professions in the city.

Landscape architects create new places of calm, places for thought or discovery, places to gather or to take refuge, or to be sad or joyful. They are the places we need as our cities and neighbourhoods grow. In Australian cities many well-known women landscape architects have re-imagined small and jewel-like local parks and squares. Our suburbs need much more of this. Jane Irwin, Kate Cullity, Elizabeth Peck and Sue Barnsley, sometimes working with artists such as Jennifer Turpin and Michaelie Crawford, Caroline Rothwell, Fiona Foley and Janet Laurence, have created magical places that tell stories or simply give shelter, calm and delight in the city. Through their work these women have begun to infuse some of the delight and urban quality of European cities into Australian cities. Their work shows how women have the capacity to renew tired spaces in an instinctive and distinctive way, bringing new life to lost parts of our cities and suburbs. There is a sense of invitation, a softness, playfulness, lushness, intimacy and femininity in many of the landscapes designed by women.

My discovery, by chance, of the Lurie Garden in Chicago on a visit to the Millennium Park was a joy. This wild scented garden of curving paths takes us through waist-high prairie grasses and wildflowers that reminded me of the childhood stories I had read of life on the prairies of Ontario. It was a charming surprise and contrasted with the shiny modern design of Anish Kapoor's *Cloud Gate*, nicknamed the Bean, and Frank Gehry's stunning outdoor concert hall and performance space, places that have now become integral to that landscape and which are greatly loved and visited. I later discovered that the Lurie Garden was the design of a woman, the landscape architect Kathryn Gustafson; at the time walking in it gave me the sense of crossing a border. The funding for the project had come from a woman philanthropist in Chicago.

Women designers and artists working on the public canvas of the city tell stories about the place and its community or about human life with a simplicity and beauty that people walking down the street who may never enter a gallery or read a history book can look at, be touched by and enjoy. Women are adept at inviting communities into the process of planning and designing. They hold difficult conversations with people sometimes resistant to the changes that might ultimately benefit their communities.

If Marion Mahony Griffin had wanted to be recognised as a great woman architect, her wish was not realised, at least not in her lifetime. But if, like many women designers, her interest lay in the end game – the creation of wonderful places – her influence and success can be claimed as being among the greatest of any woman architect. Her hands were on the design of a whole city, under the blue skies of Australia's national capital, Canberra. Although no one really knows how much of architect Walter Burley Griffin's competition-winning design for Canberra was influenced by his wife, we do know that her subtle and detailed watercolours and line drawings brought the idea of Canberra to life in ways that made the dream of a city on that flat dry plain seem real. Her hand drew and painted the exciting possibility of a garden city by a lake as a great modern twentieth-century city. Her drawings of the plan for Canberra give us a city as house and garden. It is a designed landscape for architecture to blossom. It is our national city as a stage.

Castlecrag, on Sydney's north shore, where Walter and Marion lived, was a different kind of dream of a perfect way to live as a community. The curving road they called The Parapet, circling around the hill that dropped down to the water, must have seemed a perfect landscape for their utopian, mystical way of life. The houses designed at Castlecrag still sit in their semi-bushland setting and are as appealing today as they once were. I visited the house where they lived and their spirit remains in the modest size of the rooms and the Frank Lloyd Wright-like quality of the design – or perhaps that's Marion's design hand at work.

Australia's national capital, Canberra, now just beginning its second century and Australia's only major inland city, is juxtaposed against the powerful folding landscape of the Brindabella Ranges and nestles around the lake designed into the landscape in the Burley Griffin plan. In *Cold Light*, the third book of a trilogy about Canberra's early days, Frank Moorhouse gives a fictitious account of the making of the city. It is said that Sir Robert Menzies, the prime minister at the time the lake was to be constructed, was at the last minute convinced by one of his female advisors not to axe it from the plan. It was considered an extravagance. The Griffins fought for it too. It is believed that Marion Mahony Griffin's interest in theosophy led to the carefully planned feng shui of the Burley Griffin plan with water at its centre. Without the lake the harmonious and well-balanced central focus of Canberra would not exist, and what a barren place Canberra would be.

In world studies of liveability, Canberra does well. So perhaps that is a contemporary measure of what women can contribute to city design. Working in Australia's fly-in-fly-out capital, I learned to love the strange grandeur of its buildings and its stately national monuments, the clean thin mountain air, the birdsong and the promise of farmland and bush beyond. Planned in the early 1900s, Canberra was conceptualised as a boulevard city. Landscape architects now recognise that the Griffin plan is the only plan from the Boulevard City movement to have been built, at least in part. Canberra is remarkable as a planned city and it deserves more recognition as the work of a partnership between the Griffins, Walter and Marion. A beautiful and major monument to Marion Mahony Griffin in a central public place, perhaps designed through a competition solely for female architects and landscape architects, would be a fitting, albeit belated, recognition of this extraordinary woman.

Marion Mahony Griffin resembled many women architects, in that she was a willing collaborator with the men with whom she loved to work. When she and Walter won the competition, it must have seemed an incredible opportunity to design a city for a young society halfway across the world. Chicago, where they lived, was then the city that people visited to see skyscrapers and glimpse the future.

But Walter and Marion had a different, more human, future in mind for Canberra.

Many women architects, landscape architects and planners work alongside men and make projects happen. Louis Kahn and the women in his design life offer a famous example of this. Honest architects will say it is often impossible to say who, in the creative heat and climax of designing, really has the ownership of ideas – and the best architects don't care.

The extraordinary Capitol Theatre in Melbourne with its magnificent art deco interior, designed by the Burley Griffins in 1924, is a project that architectural historians now believe was a team effort. In a 2013 exhibition to celebrate the centenary of Canberra at the National Library of Australia, titled *The Dream of a Century: The Griffins in Australia's Capital*, Marion Mahony Griffin is at last finally acknowledged as the architect she was. The curator Christopher Vernon writes about her work in Frank Lloyd Wright's Chicago office, where she worked as a young architect.

> In 1909, Wright sold his practice and travelled to Europe. The task of completing his unfinished work fell to Marion. She now took up a studio that also accommodated Walter's. Again working in close proximity she combined her practice with his.

There are many reasons that might explain why, in the twentieth century, women architects were not given the opportunity to design public buildings in cities anywhere in Australia or were not acknowledged when they did. The American architect Julia Morgan worked in San Francisco for her entire life and designed some of the city's great buildings, breaking with convention. In Australia she had no equal. In the nineteenth century women did not have a place in business and only small numbers of women then chose and had access to a university education. Now about fifty per cent of architects graduating in Australia are women. Will this see more public places designed by women in this century? Will our cities be different if we have more work in women's hands? Women architects spend many hours exploring these questions. Most architects acknowledge a gender divide in the kind of work that women architects have done. The statistics today acknowledge the situation: they show a small percentage of women registered as architects, with very few as designers of major public places, or if they are, they are working on the fine and excellent detailing, but the authorship is someone else's. The reasons for the male domination at the top of the profession worldwide are varied. Women architects still acknowledge the 'glass ceiling' has been hard to crack. Older women architects hope that with access to a different kind of education and different attitudes to professional work things will change. In the next generation surely there will be more women involved in designing cities to nurture nature and human life.

TOUGH, TALENTED AND COURAGEOUS

Everyone has talent. What's rare is the courage to follow it to the dark places where it leads.

ERICA JONG, FEAR OF FLYING

City-making is political life at its most risky, complex and intense. It is about money and competing demands and about communities and their million competing interests, and yet needing to co-exist. Harmony is the ultimate aim. Success in city-making can be seen and felt. It happens when design and the chaos of human life harmonise with grace.

Today in the battleground of building city towers a certain toughness and tenacity are required to shepherd designs through the planning process, while vigilance is necessary in overseeing the detailed design and construction to ensure that cost-cutting does not compromise the design. But women are equally capable of playing this game. The men who are best at it often adopt the tactics that mirror some of those used by women. Lucy Turnbull, as Lord Mayor of Sydney, oversaw international design competitions and major developments.

Marion Mahony Griffin was not a feminist, but her situation was unusual: in her lifetime she was a rare woman architect working alongside Frank Lloyd Wright, the leading studio of the era. It seems she was happy being there and doing the work and she didn't crave authorship. Now in the twenty-first century women deserve authorship and recognition for the work they have done. Zaha Hadid has shown

The first woman to be Lord Mayor of Sydney, **LUCY HUGHES TURNBULL, AO,** is a historian, urbanist and civic leader focused on Australia's cities.

this on an international stage, although it was years before anything of hers was built in London. Her fluid white extension to the Sackler Gallery in London's Hyde Park offers a tongue in cheek complement to the simple Georgian brickwork beauty of the low-scale gallery.

Zaha Hadid is the first woman to be awarded the Gold Medal for a body of work, in her own right, by Britain's Royal Institute of British Architecture. This is the highest honour for architecture in that country. She was awarded it in 2015, but the prize has been given since 1848. By smashing this glass ceiling she's proved it can be done to the next generation of young women architects.

There is no woman architect with Hadid's fame in Australia in the twenty-first century. Why? Older women friends tell me that in the Australia of the twentieth century it was not until the 1960s that women's formal education began to match that of men. Explanations offered by older women architects for the paucity of public buildings designed by women include the technical complexity and long timeframe of delivering major buildings, the aggressive political process and the largely male project managers, who are more comfortable working with men in what they still see as men's business. Motherhood can get in the way too.

These architects point out that in the 1940s and 1950s girls at school in Australia learned biology and bookkeeping, not the physics, pure mathematics and chemistry that gave access to courses like architecture. They say building sites were not considered places for women. The architect Andrea Nield, winner of the Marion Mahony Griffin Prize for female architects, founder of Emergency Architects in Australia and awarded the French Chevalier de l'Ordre des Arts et des Lettres, says one of her first jobs, in 1973, was on a building site at Macquarie University. She tells me women were only first allowed on building sites at around that time. When women were employed as nippers, the traditional male role of removing rubbish from building sites, the men objected and went on strike. 'The men were annoyed that they had to remove their girlie pictures and sexy calendars from their lunch rooms.' The ban meant women architects couldn't go on site for a time. She said even the Christmas gift ritual of a slab of beer caused consternation and she was given a bottle of gin! Building sites, she says, remain uncomfortable places for women.

Much has changed in terms of women's education. It is still more common to see husband-and-wife teams succeed in Australia's public architecture than to see women striking out alone as architects leading major public projects. The artist Janet Laurence, married to the leading Sydney architect Brian Zulaikha, has collaborated in a partnership of artist and architect, where each has worked on their own project. Janet Laurence says she loves the idea of working in the public domain but she doesn't enjoy the process of development and working on site with project managers. 'It is always easier, more enjoyable and more appealing to work with cultural institutions. If I work on public projects I want someone between me and the project manager.'

Clover Moore commissioned the husband-and-wife partnership of architects, the late Nick Murcutt and his wife Rachel Neeson, to design a new swimming pool complex in Sydney's inner-city Prince Alfred Park. The pool has received international design recognition and was awarded the Sulman Medal for public architecture. Surrounded by happy yellow beach umbrellas, it is a burst of joy, like a field of giant sunflowers in the park. Rachel Neeson, also the mother of young children, told me the early design work was a true partnership with her late husband. She courageously completed the project as theirs, after his death. Clover Moore praises it as 'a beautifully detailed project' by Rachel Neeson with Sue Barnsley as landscape architect. The combined pool and gardens is a major public place in Sydney, commissioned and delivered collaboratively by women, and it is a wonderful place to be, a playground for city workers and residents.

In Australia it took more than two hundred years, until the first decade of the twenty-first century, for two female architects, along with their husbands, to be awarded the architecture profession's highest award, the Australian Institute of Architects Gold Medal. The first to win this was Brit Andresen, who practised in Brisbane with Peter O'Gorman, her husband. Brit Andresen is a Norwegian-born Australian architect and was awarded the Gold Medal in 2002 for her sustained contribution to architecture through teaching, scholarship and practice, and particularly for the design of beautiful houses. The second and most recent woman to receive the award, Kerry Clare, was awarded it jointly with her husband Lindsay for a team effort in their design for the successful and acclaimed GOMA, the Queensland Gallery of Modern Art, with its community-focused spaces, on the bank of the Brisbane River. Kerry Clare is the first woman in Australia to share the Gold Medal for a body of work and for the design of a public place. A role model for young women architects, Kerry Clare has managed to have a long-term marriage, motherhood, grandchildren and a career as an advisor to governments. She has also been recognised as an equal in a way that Marion Mahony Griffin was denied a century ago. Recently Kirsten Thompson from Melbourne won the national Robin Boyd Award for a house near Hanging Rock in rural Victoria, but these top awards are still rare for women and we still notice and count the times they happen.

Marion Mahony Griffin graduated in 1894 and was one of the first women to receive a degree in architecture and one of the first licensed female architects in the world. She left a legacy of magnificent projects in Chicago. As an architect working in Frank Lloyd Wright's famous Chicago Oak Park practice, she is now credited with designing Amberg House in Grand Rapids, Michigan, and with the design of others attributed to him. It is her drawings of Wright's prairie-style houses that are now thought to have resonated with his women clients, leading to the many commissions that let his genius shine. The drawings had a sensibility that women found appealing. Her memoir, *The Magic of America*, written in 1940, makes it clear she saw herself and architecture and design as agents for social change and that the design of public places could contribute to a more democratic, progressive and egalitarian society. Her thinking was in line with Australia's modernist movement and these ideals are reflected in the design for Canberra. She understood that design and urban design could shape society as much as they could provide shelter or a place to live.

In her book *Women and the Making of the Modern House*, Alice T. Friedman writes:

> Wright's clients included quite a few strong willed women: in addition to Millard and Barnsdall, Wright designed houses for Susan Lawrence Dana, Queene Ferry Coonley, Mamah Borthwick Cheney (who would become his companion and lover) Alma Goetsch and Katherine Winkler, all of whom had deeply felt beliefs about social reform, domestic life and new roles for women in American society. A powerful fusion of feminism with the forces of change in architecture propelled these projects into uncharted realms of originality.

Although Marion Mahony Griffin fell out with Wright, she remained always utterly devoted to her husband Walter Burley Griffin and followed him around the globe.

Inseparable from Griffin in his working life, Marion Mahony Griffin worked with two of the great architects of the twentieth century as an equal. She saw herself as a collaborator in a field of individuals. Sadly, when he died she left behind her dream suburb and house in Sydney's Castlecrag to return to Chicago as a widow. Unrecognised then for her contribution to architecture, Marion Mahony Griffin was buried in Chicago in a pauper's grave. Now she is remembered in the architectural profession in Australia through the award in her name given to Australian women for outstanding contributions of all kinds to architecture and the making of great places in Australia.

The Sydney architect Louise Cox is recognised by her peers as a woman who broke through the glass ceiling, being the only woman to have been elected President of the International Union of Architects, the profession's global peak body. The words her peers use to describe her are 'strong, tough, independent and determined'. She has achieved many firsts in a still male-dominated profession. In 1988 she followed Melbourne's Dimity Reed, who was the first woman to be elected

Chapter President of the Royal Australian Institute of Architects. Louise Cox was elected Chapter President in New South Wales, going on to be one of the first women elected President of the National Council. As a young woman she was the first woman to be a partner in a large professional practice, the Sydney firm of McConnell Smith and Johnson. Louise is warm, capable and seemingly fearless and determined when situations need it. Clear in her values and willing to be outspoken and passionate, she is a role model in advocating the value of architecture and its place as a career for women. A story from one of her close friends is that while working on a major hospital project she had a new baby under the desk awaiting breast feeds! Why there are so few women like Louise Cox, who is now better known internationally than in Australia, is perplexing to the next generation of young Australian women in the design professions. She says it has been easier for a woman to find acceptance outside Australia, even though there are relatively few women at the top of the field of architecture worldwide.

More women in Australia practise landscape architecture than architecture. The strong participation of American women in this profession encouraged Australian women to become involved in the urban design of city parks and places in the 1950s. When we are looking in cities for places women have designed, the places women landscape architects have made are the easiest to find. The success and profile of women landscape architects in Australia and elsewhere are much more visible and their work shows the nurturing places women make.

KATHRYN GUSTAFSON, *a passionate designer of landscape architecture who famously said 'the sky is mine'; a role model for young women designers.*

KNITTING THE CITY

Designing places ... sometimes it is absolutely clear where to walk and to go ... and sometimes you have to search for clues ... like in life.

TERESA MOLLER, CHILEAN LANDSCAPE ARCHITECT

Women are instinctively interested in all that knits the city together at a human scale between the buildings. Women seek a holistic world, where house and garden work together. It seems no accident that women with design talent often choose the design of public places, connecting and uniting the areas between the buildings.

Women have a special relationship with community and village life. Those who work to counter poverty in third world communities tell stories of how it is the women who hold families together with dignity and purpose. It is the women who manage the village economy, just as it is the aunties in Aboriginal communities who keep families functioning, often in the harshest of circumstances. When I was a director on the board of Care Australia our programs for improving health and economies were aimed at women. Women are the glue that keeps most families intact and when allowed can be teachers and leaders in the community. Family life teaches women, whether or not they are mothers, to nurture and be aware of the needs of ageing parents, siblings or sick friends, children or teenagers. In families women are encouraged to be kind and giving, or tough and strong, according to what the situation demands.

Bridget Smyth and Helen Lochhead are Sydney architects and

urban designers who have held a series of senior design posts in government and who have taken on the task of solving some of the more challenging urban puzzles at the heart of Australia's largest city. Both are mothers, juggling family life, architecture, urban design, local politics, commissioning and advising and guiding public projects. Patience learned as mothers is useful for city-makers and the behind-the-scenes persistence and determination of these two in building inviting and attractive places in Sydney has been highly effective. Sydney's growing public art program has flowered under the professional guidance of Bridget Smyth, who believed a city of Sydney's wealth could do better with public art and would be livelier, more fun, and more liveable for it.

That women are now urban designers and landscape architects has evolved from the art of drawing and garden design in the tradition of Australia's Edna Walling, Britain's Gertrude Jekyll and America's nineteenth-century New York society landscape architect Beatrix Jones Farrand. Gardens, drawing and the pursuit of beauty were always viewed as appropriate pastimes for women. Now landscape architecture and urban design are central to reshaping and re-imagining the cities we live in and women are good at both. Urban design can mend our broken cities, transform alienating places into welcoming ones where communities gather, connect and feel a sense of belonging.

Internationally, women landscape architects have gained a great deal of visibility and recognition for the beauty and playfulness of their public projects. North American landscape architects such as Martha Schwartz and Kathryn Gustafson received international acclaim in their own right. UK gardener and designer, Maggie Jencks, the late wife of architect Charles Jencks, is another whose contribution and influence as his partner is now recognised in the design of his sensual, curvy, sculptured grassy landscapes. Teresa Moller from Chile in South America writes as only a woman could of her work:

> Sometimes I found myself like a nurse . . . healing the wounds inflicted by man.

Her landscapes seek to create a stage for nature and to disappear into nature.

When I met Martha Schwarz a few years ago, I asked why she had become a landscape architect rather than an architect; her answer was that her father and brother were architects and she needed to carve out her own space. It seems landscape architecture is a comfortable place for women to work, despite the very complex challenges involved in making public places.

Kathryn Gustafson, mentioned earlier as the creator of Chicago's Lurie Garden, is a trans-Atlantic landscape architect living in Paris, with studios in London and Seattle. She has been invited to Australia to advise on city renewal projects such as Barangaroo and Sydney Modern at the Art Gallery of New South Wales. For young urban designers and architects she is a guru, employing and encouraging young women to work in her studios. When we met she was praising the two young women in her office who combine motherhood with wonderful design work. As a citizen of the world, Kathryn Gustafson adopted a global approach before it was mainstream. She is perhaps the most recognised woman landscape architect working in the world's cities today.

On first meeting her, I felt a sense of the yin and yang, softness and strength, of her personality, a characteristic which often distinguishes great designers. To create a place and to convince others to believe in your design and to build it takes a rare mix of talent, tenacity, courage and patience. As I sit with Kathryn Gustafson in an old world style hotel in Sydney's Rocks, she leans in and speaks in a quiet American voice. She began her design life as a fashion designer as a twenty-year-old American in Paris.

> I could design anything but I want to design great places because they are enduring and where people spend their time. I was doing well in the fashion world of Paris when I heard the term landscape architect and thought that's for me. I knew I had to make landscape architecture my life's purpose. It embodied nature, art, design – it was perfect for me.

Talking over a drink at the end of her long working day, she speaks as if confiding in me. Her mother and her father were both master gardeners and her mother a great hiker across the wild Washington State landscape. She explains that her mother knew plants and how to survive in nature and that she had learned these from her. Her admiration for them both is palpable. Gustafson explains: 'I learned from her and came to landscape architecture as if prepared by childhood'. Kathryn Gustafson punctuates her ideas with wisdom and laughter. A woman of confidence and understated style, she reminded me of the long tradition of creative Americans in Paris. Gustafson is small-framed, crisp in a sharp white-collared shirt and has well-cut straight hair. She speaks with conviction: 'We are made up of every experience we have – what influences design changes constantly and what I design today is not what I designed ten years ago'.

Gustafson sees her work on the Diana Memorial in London's Hyde Park as one of her successes. She adds: 'not least because I got through the process and saw it built, which in itself is always a success'. Gustafson explains the project is about Princess Diana:

> It is about her. It is called 'Reaching out and letting in'. I really did not want a statue that you would look at. I wanted a place you could be in. She was inclusive and that's what her memorial needed to be. It had to be about the public's perception of who she was. It is for the people who remember her.

Kathryn Gustafson's Diana Memorial Fountain in Hyde Park feels feminine, graceful and sensuous, with its curves and the sweep of silvery water. It attracts crowds, who sit at its edge and dip their toes into the endless flow of water circling and falling, reminding us of the eternity of loss and of memory. On any Sunday it is crowded with happy families and children tracing the circle, splashing, playing and lazing around it. It seems it might have pleased the Princess, who loved children.

City children need places to feel the freedom to climb trees, touch the earth, skip, play hide-and-seek in the bushes and splash around in water. As a woman designer, Gustafson understands this. Her Lurie Garden in Chicago's Millennium Park reflects the prairie wilderness that once occupied the land. It is perhaps the re-imagined wild place of her childhood. The park is the kind of contemporary parkland our cities and suburbs need more of. It is a place made with the support of another woman, Chicago philanthropist Anne Lurie, who funded the project. Kathryn Gustafson is modest in claiming it as her work, saying the perennials planted freely like wild grasses and which bloom amongst inviting winding wooden paths is the work of her colleague from the Netherlands, Piet Oudolf. It is a magical place, inspired by nature and the prairie meadow flowers and grasses. Yet it is a designed place: its alluring winding paths lead us through designed nature and protect us from the man-made forest of glittering skyscrapers that is the Chicago city skyline. The garden shows an understanding that cities need wild places, even if we have to create them. She says: 'In the Lurie Garden I defined the space and what that space should do and how it should make you feel'. It feels feminine, sensory, free and light. Gustafson says what is often described as a female sensibility is design that is textural. She begins to answer my question: would our cities be different if more women were their designers?

> It is a choice about how you design and it is not necessarily only a female thing, men do it too. It is about the goal of what you are trying to achieve and how you want people to feel. It is important to have intent about making a place that makes us feel a particular way when we are in public space.

Gustafson believes that design in our cities is not just about giving people a sense of pleasure, but also that it contributes ultimately to our health, happiness and wellbeing.

If Kathryn Gustafson is the role model of urban designers who want to work on a world stage, then London-based architect Zaha Hadid is for some an architect role model who has joined the company of the men who are starchitects. Will she inspire the next generation of women architects to become involved in the design of our cities? I ask Kathryn Gustafson about the glass ceiling affecting female architects. She answers:

> The glass ceiling on women architects is totally different to landscape architecture. It is a really male dominated profession. It is historical for women to be in landscape, though designing these public places is as tough as architecture.

She tells me she hopes she is an inspiration to young women. Her advice to them is 'to believe they can do anything and feel they can control their lives'. To do this she suggests they need 'to take responsibility to make a commitment to a career'.

In Australia and across the globe there are discussions amongst architects to promote gender balance. In New York a group of women architects mounted a campaign to argue for better recognition for the work of women architects and called on the jury of the International Pritzker Prize for Architecture to award architect Denise Scott Browne a retrospective Pritzker Prize alongside her husband, who received the award decades ago. The case for her contribution to be recognised in a joint award was declined, but it shed light on the issue of equal recognition for women's work.

Jane Irwin, one of Sydney and Australia's leading landscape architects, who is respected and recognised by her peers for the quality of her studio's design work, says she was a messy student but has always been committed to her work as a designer. As we walk along beautiful Billyard Avenue, Elizabeth Bay, she stops to photograph a modest red brick building covered in creeper, admiring its simplicity. She has designed some wonderfully welcoming public spaces, like little Beare Park, a precious gem by the water's edge at Sydney's Elizabeth Bay. Her design repaired and remade it with a gentle yet knowing touch.

Jane Irwin believes there are 'political and social' reasons why women have not been the architects of cities and these are not related to the skill of women as designers. She agrees that the tradition of women in garden and landscape design makes the design of public places natural work for women. She says she doesn't enjoy the energy expended in the necessary political games and suggests this may offer a clue as to why few women are involved in the design of major public places: this process is usually a political process often played out in the media.

The award-winning Sydney architect, Andrea Nield, holds strong views about the barriers experienced by female architects. She is married to the Australian Institute of Architects Gold Medallist, Lawrence Nield. After more than thirty years as an architect, she observes that one of the great challenges for women architects is that the building industry is 'a place of entrenched misogyny, dominated by men in every part of the process of making buildings'. She believes the lack of women at the top of the profession goes beyond gender politics to gender differences in focus and approach.

> The breadth of women's life choices is so much greater . . . when women are architects they are more client focused and not so power focused. In general, they don't have the same cut-throat competitive nature as most men.

She says that in the past the technical challenge of major constructions deterred women who were inclined 'to fear the technical complexity of designing modern major buildings. Women are interested in the detail and the texture of projects and how places can meet people's needs'. She reflects on the view that many women have contributed as catalysts and nurturers to the success of their architect husbands or partners. She notes:

Ruby Madigan was a great hostess and socially well connected, supporting Col Madigan, architect of the National Gallery of Australia in Canberra and other acclaimed buildings. Penelope Seidler and Harry Seidler were an inseparable partnership in life, business and architecture.

In Australian cities the role of government architect is a powerful and influential one. The position in Sydney has history and gravitas and was created in 1816 when Francis Greenway was appointed to this position. The tradition continues. It has yet to be held by a woman. So far in Australian cities government architects have been men. As partners, Andrea and Lawrence Nield work jointly as government architects in the Northern Territory. Darwin is Australia's northern frontier city and their guidance as government architects and urban designers is needed. At the time of writing architect Jill Garner has been appointed Acting Government Architect in Victoria. This is as close as a woman has got since 1788.

Darwin is the one Australian capital city that missed out on grand nineteenth-century cultural gestures and town planning. It has always been more of a remote outpost than a city. Still a frontier town, Darwin is only now developing plans that anticipate its transformation into a twenty-first-century city. First a settlement, it later found a purpose as a defence base, and this remains a key function today, with a strong alliance recently forged between the US and Australia. Darwin's population comprises a large Indigenous community, young people, defence workers and retirees. It has the youngest average age of any Australian city and a tiny and transient population of around 70,000, with a large fly-in-fly-out population who work on the oil rigs of the Torres Straits. Far away from other major Australian cities, it is the closest large city to Southeast Asia. When you step out of a plane in Darwin, you smell and feel the air of Asia. In the past decade Darwin has seen its first really planned, transformative project, begun under the influence of a woman. Clare Martin, a former ABC journalist, was elected Chief Minister of the North Territory Assembly in 2001 and held the office until 2007. Many Australians only know Darwin as the town that was hit by Cyclone Tracey on Christmas Day in 1977 or as a kind of Crocodile Dundee tourist town. Sometimes the city is compared with Honolulu, a tropical outpost that is unlike anywhere else in the country! It is all these things, but under the bold leadership of Clare Martin as community leader and Chief Minister, a number of transformative moves added a level of urbanity to the city that had not before been imagined possible.

The master plan she oversaw delivered an attractive waterfront precinct to the fledgling city. While many design hands always contribute to a master plan, this one was guided in its detail by the hand of a woman, the landscape architect Julieanne Boustead. It added Darwin's first crocodile-free public swimming pool with a wave machine, convention centre, hotels, waterside housing and a boardwalk. The waterfront is connected to the centre of town through lush gardens of draping datura, bright hibiscus, grasses and feathery palm fronds.

Women in politics like Clare Martin who are not architects or landscape architects trained in design can contribute significantly to making changes that improve urban life. It just takes imagination! In London the 'absolutely fabulous' actress Joanna Lumley has proposed a footbridge over the Thames that will be a living green tunnel of plants – a small green surprise in the heart of the city. It's a kind of 'High Line' over the Thames – a green link across the river. It is a wonderful whimsical idea from a woman.

The way women work to achieve successes in cities is unique, unusual, unexpected . . . and the list goes on. The following story from a woman in Potts Point provides a good example of what I mean. As I was having coffee in my local café one morning, a chatty eighty-year-old woman of Prussian heritage seated on the banquette alongside me struck up a conversation. As we sat looking out at the mature flowering magnolia trees planted in a raised median strip garden bed – which make Challis Avenue a beautiful street – Johanna Read introduced herself. As a young woman, she had agitated to get the council to plant the trees that make Challis Avenue look attractive and leafy all year round, a little oasis amongst the dense apartments of Sydney's Potts Point. Johanna had worked as a nurse at St Vincent's Hospital and lived in an apartment overlooking the street, which in the late 1960s was being used as a drag-car strip. She was concerned people would be injured by the reckless driving and advocated for the council to install a median strip and plant trees. Small changes to our streets and neighbourhoods, conceived by women who decide to act, can be gifts to community life for generations to come. Women observe simple issues that require resolution and develop an idea, and have the persistence to get what's needed.

In more than twenty years of involvement in urban life, I have found that women leaders and decision-makers in local and state governments and in cultural, civic and community institutions have been willing to question and investigate the impact on communities of the complex work of urban change and how plans fit together. Cities and streets and parks in Australia are unlike the locked squares of English cities or the gated American compounds; they are places for everyone, in the spirit of Australia's classless society. Much of the architecture in cities that doesn't work is too focused on what happens inside buildings and how they look, and not on how they fit in and add to the city and its life.

America's legendary urban planner Jane Jacobs was wary of the simple pursuit of beauty in cities. She said: 'When we go after beauty too solemnly in cities we usually seem to end up with pomposity'. These are words worth remembering. Architects talk about buildings having form and function, but what they mean is places that work, look good, make us feel calm, relaxed, happy or excited, places that do what the designer intended. That's the aim of sensitive design. In the decades I have worked alongside women involved in making places, we women, as architects, designers, leaders and citizens, have argued for places designed with sensitivity.

Australia's cities are young and are still being shaped and changed. It will be exciting to see how women's hands will mould them and transform our community life in the next century as more women turn to city-making as their life's work.

Marvellous Melbourne was built as Australia's first grand planned city, with its architecture spawned by the wealth of nineteenth-century gold. Melbourne has reinvented its identity, building on the heritage of the previous century with its narrow, inner-city laneways lined with cafés to balance the soaring city towers of modern Melbourne. Sydney has its magnificent harbour, always present, sparkling aqua or brooding grey-blue, the salty coastal air and the rugged sandstone cliffs and bush. Adelaide, in settled South Australia, has its circle of green hills around the city, its expansive pale-blue desert skies and an inheritance of parklands and colonial architecture. Hobart has the charm of a place from another era; the colonial port echoes distant Europe. Canberra, the nation's capital has its mountain skies, bush, birdsong and mountain vistas as a grand backdrop to the city's monumental national twentieth-century buildings. Perth, on the far west coast, has the indigenous landscape of King's Park and the Swan River to remind us in the modern city of the bush beyond. Brisbane too, in the tropical north, where slick towers overlook the wild red cliffs of the Brisbane River, still speaks of a connection to the inland from where the river flows. Darwin, Australia's outback capital in the far north and set on the aqua-blue sparkle of the Arafura Sea in balmy tropical air, is the city that offers a bridge to the life of Indigenous Australia.

EDNA WALLING, *designer of wild gardens, who paved the way for professional women landscape architects.*

DESIGNS ON NATURE

Nature is our greatest teacher.

EDNA WALLING, AUSTRALIAN LANDSCAPE DESIGNER,

1895–1973

Edna Walling is still Australia's most famous landscape gardener. She is part of a long tradition of women making magic in the garden. Born in England and arriving in Melbourne at the age of sixteen, she began work as a gardener to earn a living. Young Edna Walling probably never dreamt of designing a public place. Her distinctive garden designs commissioned by owners of private houses and rural homesteads are often open to the public as part of Australia's Open Garden Scheme. She worked in gardens in Victoria, Tasmania, New South Wales, South Australia and Queensland and her gardens are cherished as much today as they were when they were first planted. She laid the foundations for women as landscape architects. Her biographers Tricia Dixon and Jennie Churchill in their book *The Vision of Edna Walling* describe her as 'intuitive, creative, ruggedly independent, honest, testy, gentle, unconventional'.

In 1927 she was hailed in the popular press as 'Melbourne's famous landscape gardener and a genius at her job'. The love of nature and the Australian bush underpinned her designs, as they do for many of the successful women landscape architects in Australia who have followed her. Edna Walling's gardens draw inspiration from the bush and use the traditional device of a series of rooms to make the garden appear larger and a place of surprises. Although best known for woodland planting, she was an early conservationist and a pioneer of the nationalist movement for naturalistic planting, writing extensively on environmental issues and the Australian bush. In 1947 for the *Australian Home Beautiful* she mused:

> How people can spare the time to go abroad is what amazes me. As I go tottering down the hill I wonder will I be able to see half there is to see in this country before there isn't a totter left. It is not the spectacular view, it's the plants, from diminutive ferns to the towering, forest trees, that I want to see.

She was born in Yorkshire, but Australia was the country she loved and where she died in 1974. Although she worked at about the same time as the English landscape gardener, Vita Sackville-West, creator of the magnificent white garden at Sissinghurst in Kent, Edna Walling departed from the traditional use of classic English plants, yet maintained the idea of the unfolding surprise, perennial borders and a wild overgrown mood. Her influence on steering Australian gardening away from the English country and cottage gardens to coming to terms with the soil and climate of our land is now regarded as having begun the movement to a more distinctive Australian gardening style. Her work remains an inspiration to the fertile practice of women landscape architects in Australia today, who add their creativity to our streets and parks and to the spaces between the buildings.

The nineteenth-century British landscape gardener Gertrude Jekyll was in a sense the role model who inspired many women to take up the career of landscape architecture; in America it was Mariana Griswold Van Rensselaer. Writing in an early American publication called the *American Architect and Building News*, Van Rensselaer, a late nineteenth-century critic and historian, advocated the importance of landscape architecture in America. As a female critic of architecture, she herself was a pioneer. Gardening was considered an appropriate activity for women, and the early American pioneering women used their skill in designing gardens to transform it from an art into a profession. Beatrix Jones Farrand, who lived from 1872 until 1959, took up garden design as a young woman. She lived in the heart of Manhattan Island and her family connections gave her entrée into New York Society. Her aunt was the writer Edith Wharton, whose lifelong friend was Henry James, whose novels describe the mannered life in New York and the lives of the kinds of people who would have commissioned young Beatrix Jones Farrand to design their gardens. Wharton and James encouraged Beatrix and introduced her to the wealthy clients who wanted both house and garden to be beautiful in New York – like the Europeans they slavishly copied.

Beatrix Farrand was the only woman to be a founding member of the American Society of Landscape Architects. A Beatrix Farrand Society still continues and is based at one of her gardens – Garland Farm, in Maine. Although not as well known in Australia, she had a long career, mainly focused on the east coast of the US, where she designed grand gardens for the Rockefellers, the Morgan family, the White House, the New York Botanical Gardens and Yale and Princeton.

In Britain in the twentieth century Dame Sylvia Crowe was an early environmentalist and leading landscape architect working on projects of all sizes, from the New Towns to churchyards. She had a lasting influence on British garden design and in Australia, where she designed the master plan for Canberra's Commonwealth Gardens.

In Australia landscape architects have made an enormous contribution to life in our cities and yet their work rarely draws the same public attention and acclaim as architects. One of my favourite small harbourside parks in Sydney, Beare Park has been redesigned with a light touch by landscape architect Jane Irwin. When I first came from a house and garden in Adelaide and was adapting to apartment life in Sydney's Elizabeth Bay, I very quickly discovered this neglected local treasure at the bottom of the hill. Beare Park became 'my garden' by the harbour. It is a sunny place to escape the walls of apartment life and to breathe in the northeasterly sea breezes.

Ten years ago it was an unloved, rather empty space in a beautiful location. There was a lawn, a few seats and a rather desolate old toilet block. Like faded beauty, it had kept its wonderful old bone structure of sandstone harbour walls, a deserted wharf and a collection of trees from the time it had been part of a grand garden. The remnants of this older garden remained: a cluster of windswept century-old olive trees, a towering monkey puzzle tree, a few jacarandas, a frangipani and a dotting of cabbage palms.

As I settled on the grass to read in the sun I used to wonder about the history of the place. It seemed connected to the one remaining Victorian mansion perched on the cliff top above it. Part of the park's charm is, somewhat strangely, the backdrop of eclectic architecture – apartments representing the style of almost every decade of the twentieth century. Now, the history of the place is told subtly in the park through designed photographic panels that display the lost mansions of Elizabeth Bay; these are set near an old fountain base still standing in the park.

The once-deserted wharf supports a happy team of baristas producing coffee and snacks with rustic charm. The café is low-key but meets the local need for coffee in the sunshine on a wharf looking over to little Clark Island, which floats like a child's dream in the distance.

The park is subtly designed so that it works like a series of rooms: there is a grass room for play where kids kick a ball and dogs fetch sticks, and another, a place to promenade along a sandstone boardwalk with hints of the history of the fish and wildlife of the area, engraved fossil-like in the pale yellow stone. Sandstone stairs connect with the water and to the tidal beach of Elizabeth Bay, once a sandy cove. Dogs can swim; canoers can call in. On the sun-soaked seats at the quiet end of the cove I've seen actors sip coffee and learn their lines. Placed in the thoughtful design hands of Jane Irwin, Beare Park tells its story and is a living room for every imaginable inner-urban tribe. It even has a kitchen!

Families come with toddlers to scoot along the sandstone paths or visit the playground, which has become a small person's sanctuary, kept safe by a scaled-down picket fence. Kids wade in the shallows of the Victorian fountain. Dogs love it. Groups of card-playing young men, circles of picnicking young girls and couples at every stage of life are here in this model urban park. The remade Beare Park is a perfect example of what every inner-city urban community needs, although few are fortunate enough to boast the stunning backdrop of Sydney Harbour.

The land was originally part of the Gadigal land granted by Elizabeth Macquarie's husband, Governor Lachlan Macquarie, to Alexander Macleay. The wrought-iron fountain that remains was once located in a high Victoriana glass conservatory, known as St Monan's. An early etching shows its pretty cupola sitting below a balustrade retaining wall, which is still there, as is the monkey puzzle tree, also in the etching. The garden was part of the landscaped gardens of a harbourside mansion known as 'Tudor'. Early photographs from the Caroline Simpson Library and the research collection of the Historic Houses Trust, now the Sydney Living Museums, illustrate the grand mansions that lined the foreshore in the 1880s. The story behind the garden reminds us how cities evolve and change – how they can adapt to meet new needs. This is a place that will enrich the lives of the people who will move in and out of the thousands of apartments within fifteen minutes walk of this special place remade by a woman, with another, the Lord Mayor, making it possible.

Before Jane Irwin was asked to redesign this park, it was quite small and unremarkable, except for its location. She has given the local residents a place that is exactly what is meant when planners and politicians talk about liveability and quality of life. Jane is a lively, warm, modest, yet gifted designer who grew up in country New South Wales, where her parents gave her the love of the land and of gardens. She tells me her father was a soil scientist and her mother a gardener. She clearly has a blend of their talents and interests. As a teenager she moved with them to Changmai, in the north of Thailand, where she finished her secondary school education as a postal student. What she lost in formal education she gained in an understanding of other cultures and communities. A perfect training for the thinking, problem-solving and sensitivity needed to work on making places with local communities.

Women working in the world where our cities are shaped, whether politicians or leaders, planners or policy-makers, recognise and understand how people use places in the city as their living rooms and meeting places for community life, and they care about how these places make us feel. The aim of most women is to create spaces that welcome us, like a home, and offer comfort and beauty. The women I have worked with in government have all taken a long view, as custodians of places that can improve the lives of people in their community and the strength of community bonds. Their interest encompasses more than the design of buildings and extends to the spaces beyond and to how places can make us feel and what we can learn from them – about our past, our neighbours and ourselves.

Public places tell public stories. Janet Laurence is a Sydney artist who has collaborated with many architects, landscape architects and artists in interpreting and sharing the stories of public spaces. She says her work echoes the architecture it is intended to complement while retaining organic qualities and a sense of transience. There is a generosity in her work, a child-like enthusiasm and fascination in found objects of nature, and a profound concern for life and its fragility. Despite these very female characteristics, she displays a persistence and determination to create and work in the way she sees the world.

Janet Laurence's most visited and enduring public work was undertaken for Australia's bicentennial celebrations with the Indigenous artist Fiona Foley, a Badjala woman. Known as *The Edge of the Trees*, it is a site-specific work in the Museum of Sydney and is integral to the design of the museum's forecourt, linking the building and what happens inside, to the land and place. Like a songline to pre-European days, it invites us to consider a time when the land over which the pavements and streets of Sydney now spread was inhabited by the local Indigenous people. The forecourt traces the original outline of the walls of the first Government House, linking the two histories for eternity. The work, in its simplicity, powerfully brings the symbolism of the site to any passerby's attention, reminding us of Sydney's earliest days as a city and of Australia's first people.

The diaries of the first landing describe what it was like when the British reached Australian shores, arriving in the surf and realising there were local people staring at them from the edge of the trees. Fiona Foley and Janet Laurence's trees are of steel and wood; the use of both steel and sandstone is intended to reflect modern and colonial Sydney and the timber of the trees that once stood on the site. Viewed from the café in the courtyard, the giant totems with embedded cockle shells and flotsam and jetsam from the coast bathed in the northern sun remind us of a time when Sydney was not a city. With so many layers of history in cities, the design and making of public landscaped places is an immediate and direct way to tell the story of places and their peoples to inform strangers and future generations. Even the way landscapes are planted can echo the past.

In her planting design for Sydney's Prince Alfred Park, the Sydney landscape architect Sue Barnsley has created a native meadow, using wild grasslands as an under-planting below the towering Port Jackson fig trees that line the park's edge. Dramatic native planting across the park punctuates the paths for walking and cycling. While the design gives us the feeling of the bush, the landscape plan makes the most of the sense of a grand open space, maintaining the feeling of a park in the middle of the city as a place to feel free. Yet it is a park that in reality is surrounded by three-lane main roads. Best of all, the park landscaping ingeniously protects our eyes and ears from the cars.

Sue Barnsley seems a free spirit for someone who is earthed by working with landscapes. She explains that her interest has always been in the design of exterior spaces in 'extreme landscapes and her intuitive responses to them'. She grew up in the arid climates of Adelaide and in the remote South Australian rocket range-testing town of Woomera and also in America. She explains that when she studied design, all aspects of design were taught, but it was nature and the outdoors that attracted her; her interest lay in working collaboratively with other designers. Her redesign of the park is the first major change to this seven-and-a-half-hectare inner-city park in more than a century. She explains there were some changes in the 1950s but the need to upgrade the public pool led Sydney Lord Mayor Clover Moore to a rethink of the whole park. Sue Barnsley has layered contemporary uses over the old bone structure of the original Victorian Park in a careful way. Tucked in are banks of old-fashioned swings, urban life exercise stations, basketball and tennis courts and bike-servicing points, while the playing fields and great expanse of green remain. The pool, designed by Rachel Neeson and her late husband Nick Murcutt, sits nestled, hidden from view, in a planted mound, keeping the sense of sweeping openness across the park. Only locals might be aware that it is there, but for the beckoning yellow umbrellas suggesting the idea of a poolside resort.

Landscape architects respect the history of places and the landscape: Sue Barnsley tells me that before creating the park design she read about what had happened in the park in the past, intuitively designing to include a sense of the place's past in the new plan. The planting keeps the feeling of 'country': 'When you are in there you feel like you are in a paddock, a great big green space, and we wanted to keep that feel'. Prince Alfred Park is an important patch of green for the urban dwellers of Sydney. It's a park to get fit in, to commute through, to walk the dog in, for picnics – or to lie down and read a book. There is even a restored Meeting House, once called the Field House, and a building that was one of the first childcare centres in the city. Resembling something like a small clubhouse, the building now hosts yoga and stretch classes, replacing the mothercare classes of the past.

The swimming pool is built on the site of an old pool. It is a luxurious public place of spectacular design, sitting in the landscape surrounded by mounds planted with grasses and palms, with a café and children's pool. Alongside is a planting of hundreds of new trees, which will one day soon become an urban forest. The transformation of the park took place under the watch of Clover Moore and Monica Barone. It is a rare project commissioned by two women civic leaders and designed by two women.

Prince Alfred Park, like many of the largest public gardens in Sydney, was originally a Victorian park. Typical of nineteenth-century parks and gardens in Australian cities, it was based on the London model of a city, populated by parks and commons. Prince Alfred Park was first used as a showground and once had a grand Victorian exhibition building, described by Sue Barnsley 'as rather like a Victorian lady's billowing lace skirt'.

The redesign of Prince Alfred Park shows how places can change and how they attract new community tribes. The most cherished places can still evolve and change. Sydney's Botanic Gardens, originally designed with paths for a quiet stroll amongst nature, statues and fountains, have adapted, with the paths now pounded by lycra-clad lunchtime-running city workers.

London's Hyde Park, originally Henry VIII's royal hunting ground, is now the largest public park in London and it changes constantly to meet the needs of its urban users. It is a place of many parts. It is a cycle and pedestrian route early in the morning and by mid-morning a mothers' meeting place near the playground. Later on in the day it becomes a sportsground for school children, an outdoor gym for city workers and an active commuter track to the city.

At weekends Hyde Park takes on a different character and becomes a destination for London urban dwellers, an outdoor living room, meeting people's needs for space out of doors. Parks of this scale have room for everything. They are perfect places for modern monuments and memorials, like Kathryn Gustafson's Diana Memorial, because they reach out and connect to people's daily lives. They are places to watch life and – the seasons – changing.

The women who have touched these places and transformed them softly are appreciated now and will be by future generations. Edna Walling's private gardens in Melbourne, Jane Irwin's little Beare Park in Sydney, Rachel Neeson and Sue Barnsley's renewed Prince

Alfred Park and Kathryn Gustafson's Diana Memorial in London's Hyde Park are just a few examples of the places women have made for the pleasure of others. They are examples of the way women have designed with skill and concern for the place and its community, taking care and a long view. They have layered designs on nature, inviting us into the green breathing places and nature we need in cities. The untamed bush in Australian cities makes them unlike any others and will ensure that they remain that way.

JANE GRIFFIN, *aged 24, who later as Lady Jane Franklin,*
wife of Hobart's Governor, gave the city Australia's first botanic garden.

PLACES
WE LOVE

JANE LOMAX SMITH, *pathologist, Member of Parliament, Lord Mayor and protector of Adelaide's parklands, who helped replant urban bush.*

BUSH AND BIRDSONG

*The houses had gardens filled with native
Australian plants and shrubs and air filled
with the aroma of eucalyptus.*

JILL KER CONWAY, *THE ROAD FROM COORAIN*

Jane, Lady Franklin, as she liked to be called, the wife of Sir John Franklin, Governor of the colony of Van Diemen's Land before it was Tasmania, must have been surprised when she first heard the raucous cackle of a laughing kookaburra. It was not the sweet song of a European bird. Along with the proximity of the local bush, birdsong remains one of the delights of Australian cities. The warble, the shriek, the trill, the rare tweet and the mimicking sounds of Australian birds seem to calm us amidst the chaos of city life.

Jane Lady Franklin's letters describe her fascination with the wild bush, the land and the birds and animals she found around her home at Government House in Hobart in 1837.

The battle between the bush and its creatures – the wild landscape – and the creation of civilised city life was the challenge of colonial settlement. Thankfully, the bush remains a unique pleasure in the Australian city landscape.

In Hobart Jane Lady Franklin created Australia's first public botanic garden on 130 acres of land she had bought herself; it is still a park today. She set about improving the colony and, while her husband is credited with founding the Tasmanian Society to support useful scientific study, its establishment is said to have been her idea. And perhaps it was her funds that enabled it. As Alison Alexander in her book *The Ambitions of Jane Franklin* writes: 'The finances of many of her projects are not explained, but there is little doubt that her money backed them'.

Jane Franklin is an intriguing character from our colonial history and her story is worth reading in Alexander's compelling history. She was a woman of ideas. Like Elizabeth Macquarie before her, she used the influence she had to shape the place in which she lived. Botanical and scientific discovery was the rage at that time. As a woman who would bear no children, she turned her energy and attention to science and discovery. In Hobart in 1839 she founded the first Royal Society for the advancement of science outside Britain. She called the botanic garden she founded Acanthe, which means blooming valley, and added a Greek temple as a museum of natural history, believing that these public places for everyone's enjoyment and education were needed to create a civilised society. This remains true today but the places we want have changed.

Women love gardens and making gardens. Creating a public garden was a new idea in the convict settlements of Australia at the time. More basic needs such as shelter, housing and hospitals were the priority. As a woman who respected science, Jane Lady Franklin believed that in order to tame the bush as a garden that could be enjoyed, the strange plants and insects had to be understood. This meant investigating the flowers, shrubs and bird life of Australia, the flora and fauna that was so different from the European. Even in the small settlement of Hobart at that time, she understood there was a need to live harmoniously with nature. She would be surprised to know that more than two hundred years later botanists at Kew Gardens in London are still uncovering new species of Australia's unique fauna and flora. There are still more to be discovered.

Lady Franklin, who is described in letters of the time as influential, forceful and 'really quite brilliant', lived at the exciting time when science, medicine and psychology first captured public attention. With a passion to experience new places and ideas, she was an adventurer who loved to set off on expeditions into the rugged landscape of the island. When Sir John Franklin was lost in an Arctic expedition that began in 1845, she spent years funding search expeditions to locate her husband. Finding him became a cause célèbre, one which captured the imagination of Dickens and literary and scientific London of the day.

Lady Franklin, like other early women colonists, began what continues as a fascination in Australian cities – taming the bush and embracing it. She initiated a scheme whereby she would pay one shilling for every snake collected! Not so unlike Mao Tse Tung, whose decree to his people was said to be to catch a fly and rid China of flies! In the twenty-first century in Canberra, Australia's national capital, where bush surrounds many homes, wild kangaroos are still culled to keep their numbers under control. In our cities we still live in delicate balance with the flora and fauna. In the commuter suburbs in the Adelaide Hills small ladders over the freeway's concrete traffic barriers enable koalas to cross safely.

It is the proximity of the Australian bush to our cities and the patches of bushland still in them that today set Australian cities apart from those elsewhere in the world and impart to Australians a sense that we still live close to nature. Most Australians have a deep love of bush and the outdoors, which makes them want to find ways, by planting native shrubs, trees and flowers in urban places, to keep a connection to the bush, even in our cities. When Australia's cities were first settled, the parks were designed in the traditional European style, where the aim was to add a civilising influence. Fortunately some of the bush – with its bird inhabitants – in our cities survived. Birdsong as a sound in the city connects us, momentarily, to nature. It is still exciting and relatively rare for urban Australians to hear a kookaburra laugh and somehow it is more thrilling when heard in the city. It is the sound that epitomises Australia. Kookaburras are our bird! They are heard in the early morning and last thing at night in Elizabeth Bay, as the sea glimmers golden as it stretches to the heads. Yet more often in the parks around Sydney Harbour it is the shrieking maaaa, maaaa, maaaa of the rowdy sulphur-crested cockatoos, sounding like some strange flock of mutant sheep, that is heard. Despite the soaring glass towers in major cities, we still have birdsong because we have bush.

Near Sydney's City Recital Hall, just off Martin Place, a wonderful artwork called *Forgotten Songs* by Michael Thomas Hill remembers the lost birdsong of fifty birds of Sydney Cove. One hundred-and-eighty empty birdcages dangle above the laneway, emitting the songs of the birds that have long since left the city. The birds are remembered in their names etched on the street below the cages, making the lane a small graveyard in their memory. The fleeting sounds remind us we need to respect nature and its fragility.

In Canberra kookaburras and cockatoos are part of everyday birdsong. Marion Mahony and Walter Burley Griffin gave Australia a design for a capital city with enough bush to allow its inhabitants as they go about daily life to hear a kookaburra laugh and to see the swoop of cockatoos or pink and grey galahs. With its birdsong, bush and big sky, Canberra still feels like a large country town. It has more pockets of bush than most places, making Canberra seem, despite its monumental but low-rise national buildings, the most Australian of our cities.

It seems fitting that in Australia's national capital the bush and its creatures never seem far away. The Griffins' grand design established a series of axes on which the national buildings sit. Parliament House, the National War Memorial, the National Library of Australia, the National Gallery of Australia and the High Court of Australia all look as though they have been placed like sets on a stage surrounded by a backdrop of bush – the hills and mountain peaks and rolling Brindabellas – and close by are the quiet waters of Lake Burley Griffin. Canberra is the least urban and least European in style of all our cities, with its mix of suburbs and bush and twentieth-century architecture.

In the third of Frank Moorhouse's award-winning trilogy about the making of Canberra, *Cold Light*, his character Edith Campbell Berry writes of Canberra in the 1950s:

Canberra could be a stunning distinctive city, but also one that engenders civilised values in those who live there by inviting them – through its design and architecture – to participate in great civilising ventures and entertainments and study and deeds. There are already flowering park drives, parks and sports reserves, and there are some administrative buildings that are good – looking and roomily spaced in Parkland.

Canberra was designed to be a boulevard city with vast public parks of European plantings in the inner and oldest neighbourhoods. These are contrasted by gullies of gum trees, native shrubs and grasses between the circling roads, housing and freeways. The city, though a garden city, is designed for the car, with circles of freeway to whisk you from one park-and-shop town centre to another. This was modernity. The Australian artist and activist, Robyn Archer, who has adopted Canberra as one of her home cities, once described it as being 'rather like a beautiful Japanese Geisha hiding behind a fan offering intelligence and beauty, but not in a showy way, below the surface'. Canberra, at the beginning of its second century, is considering its future growth: to become a more sustainable, less suburban and more urban community, while keeping its bush character. The community is keen to have a light rail system and more walking and cycling facilities. It seems certain that the bush landscape that Marion Mahony Griffin painted will remain, no matter how Canberra grows. A small city of just under 400,000 people, it needs to rethink how to preserve its fresh mountain air, its sense of space and the feeling of being a big country town. The bush is its great strength and the legacy of the Griffin plan is guarded by the community. The more urban and intense Australia's cities become, the more important our patches of bush and leafy green spaces become to us.

Melbourne is blessed with great parks and gardens in the city, planned in the tradition of London's great parks. Sydney Harbour has fortunately kept the bush, with national park on the inner and Middle Harbour headlands and on the small yet charming islands, the grand open coastal heath landscapes of North and South Heads and the harbourside land of the still-active naval bases. These are now sacred places in the city. As well as places with some of the earliest European history of Australia, they preserve special Indigenous sites, many of which are still hidden from non-Indigenous eyes. The spot near Camp Cove, where Australia's first Governor Captain Arthur Phillip first stepped ashore, is not even marked. It may be that because Australian cities are young we have tended to ignore our history, as if it doesn't matter as much as that of the ancient European and Asian cities, which have been settled for thousands of years. Yet here in Australia, the land is ancient, its native animals and birds and our first people are the oldest on earth.

Australian cities, particularly in their parklands and areas of remaining bush, are beginning to tell the local Indigenous history, but there are still many untold stories. In Adelaide the parks were once numbered and named for prominent citizens. Now they have a series of Aboriginal names. The names reflect another history – of our first people, the land, the bush and its creatures. Sydney's headlands have hidden sacred rock art, although some of this ancient art can be seen in the national park. Because they are sacred to the original owners of the land, many of these sites remain secret.

In the Adelaide Park Lands near Elder Park, Red Kangaroo Rock, the traditional gathering place of the local Indigenous group, the Kaurna people, has been recognised. It is still a great public gathering place for Adelaide's open-air concerts and where the first-night performance of the Adelaide Festival is often held. In 2001 the Adelaide Park Lands were given twenty-three names from the local Kaurna mob. These Aboriginal names acknowledge thousands of years of Kaurna association with these parklands.

Giving the parks their Aboriginal names, along with flying the Aboriginal flag alongside the Australian flag in the city's main square, Victoria Square, was suggested by Jane Lomax Smith, as a symbolic act of reconciliation. Jane Lomax Smith was a civic leader who embraced reconciliation ahead of many others. The flag was first flown in Victoria Square during NAIDOC week in 1971 as a temporary gesture. Jane wanted it to be not just a temporary nod of respect but a permanent shift in thinking. Having been to an early reconciliation forum at the time of Australian Prime Minister Keating's Redfern speech, she convinced the council to fly the flag and it has been there ever since. It flew in Adelaide before the reconciliation walk across Sydney Harbour Bridge in 2000.

Jane Lomax Smith, an English woman and doctor who chose Adelaide as home, had a great fascination with the bush in the city and planted thousands of trees, which have now grown into a forest. Consistently rejecting any form of development in the Adelaide Park Lands, Jane argued for their protection on many occasions, recognising the threat of development, which continues to this precious green belt today. Sadly, she no longer held public office when a monolithic stadium was built on the site of the historic Adelaide Oval. There was no one to urge the men of power and influence in sport and politics to construct the stadium in a less beautiful corner of the parklands.

Jane Lomax Smith continued as a local politician for over twenty years and one of the ways she kept in touch with her supporters was to provide them with eucalypt seeds. These they could nurture and grow at home before joining her at regular working bees in what were then the desolate and cleared parklands near West Terrace in Adelaide.

Jane Lomax Smith arrived from England intrigued by science and Australia's wildlife – from its plants to its rare sea dragons. Her seedling project of twenty years ago is now an urban forest and just one of her gifts to her adopted city. This is her lesser act of kindness to the parklands and to the Adelaide community. Her constant watch and opposition prevented a grandstand and event centre being built in the East Park Lands, which would have threatened a horse racetrack still used today, its Victorian grandstand and the towering giant gums that circle the track. Of real significance in Jane Lomax Smith's protection of the parklands was her courage in opposing the development being proposed by the government in which she served.

She took the rare step of excluding herself from the inner government circle, which was intent on supporting major development for events and car racing through the park. She determinedly represented the interests of the community and the local parklands preservation group activists to halt the development. In effect, her advocacy to stop development on the parklands ended her political career. It is a noble example of a woman's courage and adherence to principle and a demonstration that she acted for the community rather than from self-interest.

Adelaide, with its hot summers and runs of days over 38° F, would be a much less pleasant place to live without its green belt and birdsong. Recognising how much we need green open spaces in our cities, it is incomprehensible why some in Adelaide consider that the removal of a few giant eucalypts wouldn't matter. The battle to preserve or develop the Adelaide Park Lands seems far from over and will always require vigilance, despite legislation and despite what sense suggests. My hope is that there will always be strong women with common sense to lead the community battles.

The former publisher, now urban planner and activist, Stephanie Johnston, is another Adelaide woman who has been a strong voice for the preservation of the Adelaide Park Lands. She is now advocating and managing the bid for the Mount Lofty Ranges to achieve UNESCO World Heritage Listing. Her aim is to ensure that the ring of green hills will always surround Adelaide and remain the food bowl it has been since Adelaide was first settled. Vivacious, quick-witted, feisty, focused and a skilled communicator, Stephanie has all the attributes of an effective activist. Perhaps one day she could be another Lord Mayor of Adelaide, although she has already taken on the role of an influence in civic life in her work as an advocate for planning reform. In a simple stroke of serendipity an Italian academic posted to one of Adelaide's universities is a woman who worked on the successful UNESCO World Heritage Listing of Bethlehem. She is sharing the experience of how to navigate the long process with Stephanie, who is determined to succeed in gaining the recognition for the Adelaide

Hills that has already been bestowed on the Tuscan landscape in Italy.

All cities and landscapes need vigilant and collaborative community activists. Adelaide would be a less attractive city without its heritage architecture, its surrounding hills and farmland, and the natural bush of the parklands. It must be one of the few cities of more than a million people with horses grazing in bush only fifteen minutes walk from the city centre. In the 1930s cows also grazed in the parklands. In North Adelaide, in a park known locally as the 'Horse Parklands', horses graze under the gums. This is a city park where much more than that happens, including tennis and other sports, running, walking, dog walking, yoga, teenage dating and children's play.

But in the park itself you have a sense that you are in a bush paddock as you look across to the Adelaide Hills in the distance curving around the city. Schoolgirls play hockey there and then meet friends. Young mothers take their small children there to talk to the horses and run free as if in the country. The ring of city parklands of bush around the city gives a sense of easy access to the outback beyond, one of Adelaide's charming features as a city. The local pink-and-grey galahs congregate in the parklands under Adelaide's desert-blue skies on any morning. Like old men out for a potter in the sunshine, they stay close to the parkland bush, scratching about in the dirt, as if they are looking for a dropped coin. Without the park, the birdsong of Adelaide would be little more than the urban call of immigrant birds like the noisy mynah birds, cooing pigeons and tweeting starlings and sparrows.

Since 1836 Adelaide has held onto the precious belt of parkland that was drawn in English town planner Colonel William Light's original plan for the city, which is said to have inspired Olmstead's competition-winning design for New York's Central Park. While the bush on Sydney Harbour seems safe from development, Adelaide's eucalypt-edged parklands are still regularly under threat from one proposal or another.

Park life happens in all Australia's major cities. Sydney's glorious

Centennial Park is just a kilometre or two from the centre of Australia's metropolis of over four million people. Here community life takes place around the clock, from dawn to dusk, as in Adelaide, although the horses don't graze freely. The Sydney horses are ridden in a circuit shared by runners and cyclists, dogs, and children, mothers and babies, all finding space in the living room of the park.

Sydney is looking at its harbour-edge bush with fresh eyes. A new plan of management for Sydney Harbour National Park was developed through consultations with the Sydney community on how to preserve but still allow enjoyment of these precious remaining areas of bush around Sydney Harbour. Margaret Bailey, a committed environmentalist who spent her whole career caring for and managing the wildlife of the national parks in Sydney and New South Wales, was single-minded in her commitment to producing a master plan that would enable the protection and conservation of these rare urban bushland parks and harbour islands and the even rarer remnant plant, bird and animal species, including fairy penguins, bird colonies and native marsupials. The plan at the same time needed to enable the Sydney community and visitors to gain easy access to the landscapes. In the past, conservationists have been wary of people using the park for enjoyment, worried they would damage rare species and bush. As Sydney has grown, these rare parklands are needed more than ever for recreation and as a balance to city life. Like heritage buildings, their structure and role need to be rethought every so often to ensure they stay protected but are also part of contemporary urban life.

The Australian bush is often associated with the rugged men who explored Australia's interior; in cities, on the other hand, women as volunteers and activists have done much to save and care for patches of 'urban' bush. Two sisters – the Bradley sisters – from Mosman, Sydney's North Shore harbourside suburb near the wild and magnificent headlands of harbour bush, were pioneers in bush-regeneration methods, which are still used today to re-establish lost native bush. Joan and Eileen Bradley, who were well known in their local neighbourhood, walked the bush at Chowder Head and Ashton Park. They began their work with record keeping in the early 1960s and, by the 1970s, with the burgeoning of the environmental movement and the notion of bush regeneration gaining political support, their work began to be acknowledged. The work and story of the Bradley sisters is told in *Bringing Back the Bush: The Bradley Method of Bush Regeneration (1988)* edited by Joan Larking, Audrey Lenning and Jean Walker. This collaborative work by many women immortalises the work of the two sisters who cared about saving the bush. By 1975 the National Trust was advocating bush conservation in the city and calling for areas to be protected as national park.

Another Sydney woman, the late Caroline Simpson, a philanthropist, is well known for her interest in and support for preserving and sharing Australia's early colonial art and history. Although she is less well known as a strong voice for national parks, her daughter Emily Simpson says she was active at the highest political levels, to which she had entrée, urging for the creation of national parks around Sydney.

One of Perth's great assets as a city is King's Park, visible on the hill from the towers of Perth's main street, St George's Terrace. It is justifiably a source of great local pride as a natural landscape almost in the heart of a modern city. Fifty years ago women volunteers, working as gardeners and propagators of seeds, began the work of re-establishing the native plants and wildflowers that had been lost to the park. Their legacy is a place enjoyed by thousands every day. Now the park continues a volunteer garden program, which assists with the maintenance of the park as well as teaching people the kinds of native plants that can be grown at home in an arid climate. The Pioneer Women's Memorial, at the heart of King's Park, contains the serene and strong monumental sculpture of mother and child created in 1968 by Perth artist Margaret Priest.

Adelaide also has a garden made by women that celebrates the pioneer women. Adelaide's charming Writers' Week is held each year in a small garden, known as the Pioneer Women's Memorial Garden, at the back of the city's Government House. As a simple outdoor room designed by women, it seems fitting that the audience is normally comprised of more women, with their shading straw hats, than men, who gather to hear the ideas of the writers of the moment from across the world. Landscape architect Elsie Cornish was commissioned by the Adelaide City Council in 1941 to create the garden to contain a sculpture of a standing woman by artist Olga Cohn. In 2036, two hundred years on from Adelaide's settlement, a time capsule in the pedestal of the work will be opened to deliver messages to the women of the future. Across Australia pioneer women are collectively honoured but not often with their individual stories told.

In the hilly outskirts of Perth, the Araluen Botanic Park describes itself as heaven in the hills. An extraordinary valley with a microclimate in which European gardens flourish, it became a public park, in the 1990s. Founded in 1929 as a holiday camp, Margaret Simons is honoured for her early planting and care of the garden that she and her husband created. As a public park today it hosts a rich array of activities to engage the local community, including a tulip festival, a chilli festival and a violinmaker's studio, which is housed in a historic cottage in the park. Araluen now has support from government but the volunteers remain its protectors.

Australians make the pilgrimage to London, Dublin, Glasgow, Edinburgh and other Europe cities to trace their heritage. As the first city of Australian settlement Sydney should join these as a special place in the hearts of Australians. It has Australia's first row houses, which still remain in the Rocks, and the finest colonial sandstone architecture. Melbourne, built on the wealth from the Victorian goldfields, has always been grand. It was the first city of ordered streets and gracious buildings, a city with all the modernity of Victorian invention and grand architectural flourish. The state ballroom of Government House is reputed to have been the largest in the British Empire at the time, even larger than the state ballrooms in Queen Victoria's palaces! Melbourne has a rich history – the Eureka Stockade, the rush to the goldfields and bushrangers – but it does not have the layers of the convict history of Sydney and its story of discovery, colonial rule and the haphazard development that came with being Australia's first place of European settlement. Not until I lived in Sydney did I understand the extent of the city's rich layers of history. The harbour bush, with its historic fortresses, is a place to roam and to learn about our country's history, about first settlement and the beginnings of Australian urban life. In the future it will also offer visitors more information about early Indigenous history. Sydney Harbour, the Rocks, Goat, Cockatoo, Rodd, Shark and Clark islands all have stories of Australia's first communities of European Australians – of the convicts, their keepers and how they lived in early Sydney town. And these are places where the first people, the Gadigal people of the Eora nation, fished and lived with nature.

National parks were created following community calls for places of natural significance and historic importance to be preserved and managed for future generations. Although women were not alone in advocating for national parks, their voices were loud and women founded and organised the first volunteer groups to begin the work of ridding the parks of pests and weeds, groups that continue today.

There is little bush in the centre of Brisbane. The lace-like pepper trees of New Farm in the gardens of the remaining old Queenslanders, with their shading verandahs like great eyelashes, remind us of country homesteads in the city.

Alice Springs, in Central Australia, may one day be a city. For now it is the most remarkable town where no amount of settlement will distract from the ridges and cliffs, the eucalypts, the desert air and sky, the sounds of insects and birds, the red earth and the dry Todd River bed. It's a place to visit if you get the chance. Olive Pink created the first botanic garden, a desert garden on the edge of the town with the MacDonnell Ranges in the distance. It is a place still used for sharing knowledge of the desert, bush tucker and the medicinal healing plants, and is sacred land.

As cities grow and change, they continue to need places where people can touch nature. The old colonial townships of Parramatta,

Penrith, Campbelltown, Blacktown and Liverpool in western and southwestern Sydney were first settled in the time of the Macquaries. Parramatta, a first seat of colonial government, is being reborn as a regional city in the west, as was once imagined. Elizabeth Macarthur's farmhouse remains there as on open-house museum showing how this early pioneer woman and leading pastoralist's wife lived. The *Australian Dictionary of Biography* describes her as 'the first woman of education and sensitivity to reach the colony'. 'Elizabeth Farm' is described as 'an impressive achievement of feminine strength enlivened by Mrs Macarthur's wit, high spirits and her intelligent interest in the development of colonial society'.

Now western Sydney has people from more than sixty different language groups and a population in 2015 of close to two million people. This community has its own vast parkland and a few women helped with its establishment. As a growing community, where increasingly many will live in apartments, this park can help to meet the community's need for a place to connect with nature and for recreation; with it, a twenty-first-century parkland has been born. The landscape architect, Suellen Fitzgerald, was appointed as its first CEO and she has been a force in the creation of this multi-use recreation space in Sydney's west.

Western Sydney Parkland is a place imagined by women. A former member of parliament for Western Sydney and Minister assisting the Planning Minister, Diane Beamer, first grasped the potential of the creation of a vast belt of parkland in this part of Sydney, amalgamating farmland and bush that had been acquired by the government over many decades. She supported the work on a parklands master plan for the land on the Cumberland Plain around the Penrith River. A land bank of 5280 hectares, stretching over twenty-seven kilometres from Quakers Hill to Leppington, has now been reserved as Western Sydney Parklands.

Suellen Fitzgerald and I worked together on the early vision for the park. She is a striking redhead with a relaxed and friendly manner that belies her determination to get things done and to give communities places to connect with the land. Suellen's childhood was mobile and part of it spent in Singapore, where, she says, she 'learned to love the exotic design, scents, culture and people of different places'. Early studies in science, marine biology and the environment led her to study landscape architecture. About landscape architecture as a career she says:

> The great thing about landscape architecture is the connection between the environment and people. What I have always been interested in is how people in cities can react with the bush, with nature and the environment.

Creating the Western Sydney Parklands is a bush-restoration project on a grand scale. Suellen says of the park today: 'Its strength is its size and the scale of it. It is twenty-five times the size of Sydney's Centennial Park and it is flexible for the long term. Its size will enable its uses to adapt to community needs now and in the future'. Since not all of it is pristine bush, it will be a place for the community to have their own vegetable gardens, while some of the land can be used commercially for market gardening and agriculture and sporting activities, raising income for running and further developing the park for recreation and public parks. She imagines it will take fifty years for Western Sydney Parklands to be a new destination for city dwellers. 'It is only twenty per cent in its final form and it is going to be a long Darwinian evolution.'

Australia has its native flowers, bush and birdsong in the open air. Singapore has a new kind of botanic garden under glass – Singapore Gardens by the Bay, which could be described as the antithesis of bush in the city. For Singapore it's a new way to give people an old experience. Its popularity highlights the need to connect with nature as cities and communities become more urban. Man-made super trees dominate the approach to the 'garden'. They are a forest of steel, lit at night with their own energy and giving back to the grid while collecting water from the sewer, purifying it and using it to water the public gardens. The tiny island of Singapore has become a metropolis in which inventive design gives new buildings and the city a sense of place. Singapore's tropical public gardens have always been a valuable connection to nature for locals and visitors. This garden is something else entirely: a brave new world of plants from faraway places and times.

This is garden as museum, and the curatorial approach to living plants is scientific. It is a giant conservatory housing plants from every region on the planet. Wandering, not unlike Alice in a strange world, you see Australian arid-land baobab trees transported far from home. There are Asian oriental lilies and orchids, bright camellias, and azaleas like butterflies, all arranged in the decorative manner of Chinese gardens. There is a stand of Spanish olive trees; one of these is a thousand years old and has been transported from the sun and wind of Spain to the controlled environment of Singapore. I mourn for its loss of freedom. The landscape of city towers is visible in the distance through the glass. The place is a strange living museum of temperate plants and perhaps meets the same need for a connection with plants and bush for the high-rise apartment dwellers of Singapore that the parklands and bush give Australians.

The use of Australian native planting by our landscape architects and the preservation of bush in the city is an important way for Australian cities to hold on to the special wild connection to nature. We need to thank all those armies of women who have been activists for the protection of bush in our cities, our grandmothers and aunts who spent their weekends planting trees along roadsides and where the bush was thin. There is still plenty to do in the national parks that surround our urban lives and they need young energetic volunteers to continue caring for the bush. Mostly they need people of courage to continue to be vigilant, to speak out and to ensure our cities gain rather than lose their precious bush and parklands and keep the optimistic sound of birdsong.

SECRET GARDENS

A garden is as unruly as people are, it does its own thing
no matter what you might want.

WENDY WHITELEY

The madness of city life means we need to experience nature close up and find quiet places to which to escape. Secret, hidden gardens are a refuge in the city when we find them. There's a difference between urban parks and wild gardens. In earlier days they converged in a municipal model, which gave us showy flowerbeds and the secure sense that we could tame the wild nature of the Australian bush that lurked outside the city. Now we yearn for that wilderness in the city to counterbalance the packaged order of modern city life.

In the centre of most Australian cities we find European-style parks as the model and reminder of the more gentle life lived in the last century. The public gardens in St George's Terrace in Perth, Hyde Park in central Sydney and the showy seasonal flowers on the banks of the Yarra in Melbourne and along Adelaide's Torrens River are reminders of palace gardens or cottage gardens. Grand or mass-planted beds of seasonal flowers, beautiful to wander through, are a reflection of a European construct of cities and order. Many of these gardens are being replanted with less water-hungry Australian native grasses, almost like cultivated weeds. Too often the focus is on showiness – on places to look at and pass by rather than linger in and relax.

Some of the best gardens are in the hidden places in cities and are created from abandoned and derelict spaces. Wendy Whiteley

WENDY WHITELY, *wife and muse of Australian artist Brett Whitely, who gave Sydney's Lavender Bay a secret, joyful garden for everyone to share.*

and Gaye Porter are Sydney artists who have worked on lost, ugly or abandoned places and given them new life, dedicating years of their lives and their hearts and souls to the task. Sunday Reed gave Melbourne her simple and now famous garden, Heide. These women have all applied their own artistic sensibility to making places for others to enjoy, a sensibility not concerned but perhaps delighted by the unruly, random flowering.

When sculptor Gaby Porter worked in Bennett Place in inner Sydney's Surry Hills, she yearned for more space for working on her metal and ceramic sculptures. The small internal studio in an old factory no longer met her needs as an artist. She explained: 'It wasn't the answer and I went searching for an escape from the city'. In 1995 she found what she calls a 'scrappy block of land' between the soaring cliffs of Coaldale and the beach on the coast south of Sydney. It is close to where D.H. Lawrence wrote the novel *Kangaroo*.

A small and sunny woman, Gaby seems almost too tiny to have produced some of the great metal works that inhabit her garden. But her hands are working hands and she speaks with these strong-fingered hands. She tells of her love of shapes, explaining that her father, as a pioneer of animation in the Australian film industry in the 1930s, too loved shape and design. His work fascinated Gaby as a child and continues to inspire her, with her work lovingly exploring shape and form. Ordered neatly in her outdoor studio are groups of similar shapes and forms, in rows and clusters of different tones and materials – ceramics and metal.

In the garden below she's made birds and creatures that have names and personalities. They nest in the rainforest as though they had been put there by nature's hand. A floating metal cup – a fountain – sits like a lily pad on a pond. Magic mushrooms and red forest-floor fungus made by her are scattered on bare earth. Ceramic and metal birds nestle lightly in the ferns alongside bright-blue enamel poppies, bursting like true flowers in a patch of sunlight cutting through the trees. Twigs are gathered and transformed – a tepee or a nest of russet twigs. Once sticks on the rainforest floor, they have been gathered to make an elegant shape. A solitary stone pelican, neat in its nest, keeps watch. Female forms and reminders of fertility fill the garden. Big blue bowerbird eggs in a giant nest nestle in a clearing.

Shapely nudes, scattered eggs, rounded forms of every kind, even families of shaped stones are lined up in rows. It seems that little in the rainforest is not inspiration or material for Gaby's artful eye. There's an intensity and drive in her aqua-blue eyes, and the child who so loved her father's animation is clearly still playfully exploring in the garden and making her own fantasy creatures.

When Gaby arrived in Coaldale, what is now the sculpture garden at Wombarra was a run-down property. It contained a dilapidated miner's cottage, more than a hundred years old, and a series of basic cabins. 'The land was muddy, with leaches, and an old tip remained; the rat-infested land had been invaded by lantana, privet and weeds, weeds and more weeds.' In amongst the overgrown and degraded seven-hectare block were a few small patches of the rainforest from the pristine landscape of the Illawarra escarpment, between what is now the Royal National Park and Wollongong.

For Gaby the small patches of rainforest promised what might be possible in her Wombarra Eden. Today, more than a decade after she first began reclaiming the land as rainforest and bush, the Wombarra Sculpture Garden is a quiet haven, which she opens each month as a public garden for others to share and enjoy. 'I feel like a young bride every month welcoming people to the garden.' The garden imparts a particular serenity the moment you enter its stillness. Although only minutes from the Pacific Highway traffic and just an hour's drive from the fury and pace of Sydney, it's a magical place, one made for others to enjoy. It's not surprising that people connect deeply with the hillside garden set beneath the protective soaring, jagged escarpment; here the rambling, random and shaded paths and its scattering of Gaby's playful toy-like sculptures invite discovery. The whoosh of the nearby waves is like a soothing soundtrack amongst the birdsong of the garden. The sounds and the spirit of the place remind me of a Peter Sculthorpe quartet.

People come and they do connect. We can so easily lose touch with the real world. Beauty has become a bad word these days, but it should not be, we all long for it. When it comes to creating art I love the beautiful shapes. I find I can't stop work in the garden. I get excited and I can't sleep and tell myself not to think and to empty my head!

Gaby believes trees have an energy that we can feel. Her life at Wombarra as a practising artist is her work, and is a life she wants to share. She doesn't see the sculptures or the garden as a business, but rather as a life for which she needs enough money to live – but not to be rich.

In the freedom of her garden she has left behind the dictates of gallery owners. 'It is so important to keep your heart in your work as an artist – or in whatever you do – if you are half-hearted that's what you get.' Her mission as an artist is to create beauty and harmony that move people. 'I want this place and my work to be about feeling, intuition and the unspoken.' For Gaby there's an energy and urgency to continue the task of making the garden and the work that is placed so beautifully within it. A place of fulfilment and contentment for sharing with others, the Wombarra Garden is a reclaimed dump, not unlike the exquisite garden that Wendy Whiteley has given Sydney on the hill above Lavender Bay, which her famous artist husband's work immortalises.

I first wandered into Wendy Whiteley's garden years ago before it had been shared with the Australian public on television. On a cold winter afternoon when I was walking a happy Labrador belonging to a friend, I stumbled on it, unaware of the story of the stolen garden. It is a rambling garden of paths and stairs, offering glimpses of aqua-blue harbour, boats and the arch of the bridge. Living in the eastern suburbs of Sydney is a bit like living in quite a different city from that of Sydney's North Shore. So as I set off to walk the dog in a suburb I didn't really know, I was unsure of what I would find. I was drawn down to the harbour. I knew from Brett Whiteley's Lavender Bay series that this was the part of Sydney he and his wife Wendy had made home. I had often looked across at Luna Park and the little bay alongside, with its small bobbing boats, but never made the trip to explore it. The Whiteley story is a legend of love, life on the edge, living for art, and freedom. It is a particularly Sydney story. I had often visited Brett Whiteley's studio in the small terrace of Surry Hills, which is now a museum of memory for the artist, his life, genius and work. Sydney is full of steep stairs but I have learned they are always worth climbing or descending because the end point never disappoints. The first day I visited Wendy Whiteley's garden I followed the eager, exploring Labrador, bottom wiggling. The dog's instinct was good. There was fun to be had at the bottom.

I passed the Whiteley house with its Rapunzel-like tower at the top, a fairytale idea adding magic to the turreted Edwardian house overlooking the bay. The first hint of the garden is an oversized, proud African head, a smooth stone sculpture under the shade of a giant Morton Bay fig. The land drops to the water and paths draw us into the garden. On this first visit I was not aware of the garden and did not know its story. I learned it was a garden made with the ache of love and loss. On that first visit the love with which it had been created could be felt. Afterwards I asked Sydney friends about it. Later I watched the ABC's *Australian Story* documentary, in which Wendy Whiteley walks in the garden and describes how claiming what was a desolate no man's land left to decay by government had healed her grief. Working each day with the soil had enabled her to face the long and endless processing of grief from the loss of her daughter Arkie and her husband, her soul mate. She enlisted the help of others to dig and plant and place found objects, using old garden furniture in the garden rooms as they were created. Wendy Whiteley says: 'Life is what we've got and our imagination and creativity. That's all we've got really. I see the garden as alchemy, my alchemy, to me alchemy is the best of what one does.'

The garden brings Bali to mind, as well as the work of Brett Whiteley. It has tranquility, the sense of jungle with terraces and paths that lead labyrinth-like, calming the walker. When the garden was first established there was no 'official' recognition but it is now recognised and cared for by the North Sydney Council and enjoyed by anyone who wants to wander in. It is a gift from a woman to strangers.

Known as The Rose, singer Bette Midler made her first city garden in 1995 on what was a desolate windswept railway yard at the edge of the Hudson River in New York. Bette grew up in the lush green of Hawaii and its flowering trees. She has made many gardens since that first one, which began as a project for homeless people who worked on turning urban ugliness into welcoming beautiful places in a city neighbourhood. The legacy of the first garden is a not-for-profit organisation dedicated to developing and revitalising parks, community gardens and public spaces in New York City. With the help of corporate, community and the US National & Community Service Americorps volunteers, tons of garbage have been removed from abandoned sites in Manhattan to make way for community garden projects. The mission of the Divine Miss M has been to save these precious undeveloped spaces from being developed and to add to the city a network of gardens and grass, to enable people to have places where they can touch the earth.

Bette Midler's New York Restoration Project supports projects across New York, from East Harlem to the West side. The projects create safe places for children to play as well as local gathering places where the community can learn about gardening and plants and caring for the land. She is well recognised in the US for this gift. In an interview with the online *Huffington Post*, she says of her childhood in Hawaii:

> Most of the families worked for the military or out in the sugar cane fields. But even though people were poor, when you walked out of your crappy house you were rich – because the sky was crystal clear and the waters were full of these jumping fish and everyone had gardens.

She describes how people worked hard to make the land extraordinarily beautiful, with its Japanese gardens and the regular pruning of the public trees. Her philosophy is not just to be fair to human beings; we must be fair to the land too as part of a greater cycle.

On the outskirts of Sydney's western suburbs, at Fairfield, a group of women worked together on a project called Restoring the Waters, the aim being to return a revitalised river and a park to its community. The Restoring the Waters project grew out of a study by landscape architect Barbara Schaffer into concrete drains across the suburbs of Sydney. These were once natural waterways which had been allowed to deteriorate or had been cemented over into drains. Barbara approached councils with a project for returning them to streams. Fairfield Council took up the idea and, with public funding intended for river restoration, established a public art project, called Restoring the Waters, involving the local community.

Two artists, Jenny Turpin and Michaelie Crawford, created a plan to work with the local community on this project. These two women, who work with nature, are best known for their giant steel sculptures that move unpredictably in response to the energy of wind or water and balance and play in the public urban spaces where they are 'planted'. The first stage was called The Memory Line. By planting a sinuous line of wheat on the course where the river had once run, the team of women inspired the community to re-imagine the existing no man's land and the ugly concrete drain as a natural waterway in a park lush with bush and bird life, natural stones and a wandering stream of water. The landscape architect, Sue Barnsley, then designed the returned river. She described to me the sense of sadness the community had felt at the loss of the river the day the concrete drain replaced it.

Discussing the work, Jenny Turpin speaks gently and quietly: 'When we work with communities we often give them back a memory of something that was lost or we ignite a memory'. With the planting of the curving river-like thread of grasses across the barren park behind the suburban back fences, the possibility of a waterway was made real. Jenny Turpin says:

Now it's a place that people like to be; an oasis in a suburban area where people can fish and potter and touch the earth and water.

Jenny Turpin and Michaelie Crawford also designed an elegant sculpture in an urban garden on another industrial inner-Sydney city site, which is now a desirable address. *Halo*, in Sydney's Chippendale, is an elegant steel sphere suspended on a ceramic ball bearing the size of a marble. Metres high and reflecting the sacred geometry of the circle, *Halo* floats above the park below, sways and moves 'turning and tilting with the energy of the wind'. The project created an object of beauty in the courtyard of what was once an industrial brewery site. It is now a new city village of apartments, designed by men who are recognised as amongst the leading architects of our times. The vertical village has been designed by Jean Nouvel's studio, in France, and Sydney architect Richard Johnson and his studio. However, it is the graceful work of Jenny Turpin and Michaelie Crawford that is at the heart of the village, with *Halo* imparting a feminine fluidity and softness to the towering glass of the place. Jenny agrees she works in a world populated more by men, who don't always find it natural to be working with women, commenting:

> They see us as different creatures. One day when we were arguing for a design at a particularly tricky point, we overhead the project managers saying to each other: 'Ok, look out here come the lionesses'.

Cities and communities need quiet places to reflect. Imagination and belief turned these blighted, unused places into the loved and welcoming places that are much needed by their urban communities. Women artists and designers recognise that we need beauty in everyday life. They have the imagination to create magic from ugliness and abandoned places. These gardens and landscapes began as dreams. Now they are real places made for strangers with love.

URSULA HAYWARD,
whose home, Carrick Hill, is now a house and garden for everybody.

HOUSE AND GARDEN

Cosmopolitan society is like taking a journey
without moving.

COCO CHANEL

Women continue to create places for sharing that reflect their ideas about life and how we should live. House museums are special places, where collections and memories are shared and strangers are invited into another's life, to walk in their shoes. In our connected modern world we can now Google and look, like Alice down the rabbit hole, with curiosity into other worlds. But nothing is quite like stepping physically into the once-private world of another person's life.

Living museums are important for the curious, the urgent young, the old with time on their hands, for all of us who are making sense of the past and the future, and of how the two are linked. They teach lessons about how to live, about possibilities we may not have known about. The rise of social media shows that people are vitally interested in other people's stories and in the way they live.

Sydney's much-loved artist Margaret Olley, who lived the last decades of her life in Paddington, painted the domestic life world around her in the home that became the canvas of her life. She clustered her favourite objects – vases of flowers, teapots and glasses – to immortalise her life in art. Her paintings reflect her preoccupation with her own domestic world. During the last years of her life, her home in Duxford Street, Paddington, was her studio, her sanctuary, her stage and her salon. It was a place of refuge, where food and art and friends and painting and the ephemeral collections of her life, all coexisted in a way that people close to her loved and relished.

Now the home that was at the heart of the work and life of Margaret Olley will be shared with anyone who cares to visit. Her living room has been painstakingly moved and recreated with love by women who were her admirers and friends. This is not a house museum rather a window to her life located in a gallery she had always supported – in the northern New South Wales town of her childhood, Tweed, near the Queensland border, a place the artist loved.

This great Australian still life artist was a Sydney treasure. She was witty and whimsical and with a presence that grew with age. Warmth and love for life and beauty radiated from her. When out, she dressed as if for a portrait sitting, with hats and glittering scarves, bright colour snoods, beads and bangles; she was bohemian and beautiful. She was often at gallery openings at the Art Gallery of New South Wales, a place that she loved and to which she gave most generously. When meeting her, it was obvious that she loved life – she was often the last to leave a good party. One evening when a friend at my table at a dinner in the Art Gallery of NSW won a magnum of red wine in a raffle, Olley wandered over in a childlike but determined way and asked if she could have the bottle once the contents had been consumed. To Margaret Olley objects were for collecting, props to study and perhaps paint. She was a bowerbird who saw beauty in ordinary everyday life and the things that surrounded her. People who didn't know her well, but whose lives her work touched, loved her, even those who might not have loved the colourful still lives, with their chaotic colour and sliding perspective. Stories abound in Sydney about the many younger artists she helped by buying their work and giving it to galleries.

Many Australian women have been philanthropists, giving to and enriching cultural places in our cities. Sometimes they leave their houses or their collections. Women who share their life's work and passions, whether collecting, painting or gardening, share their lives with strangers, an act that gives them a kind of immortality. For their sense of intimacy I love house museums, perhaps more than many grand formal and more significant collections. We feel a connection to the women who have opened their houses and, with them, their hearts. Small living museums and houses are wonderful places for people in the twenty-first century to visit because they offer a window into a world before cyber space. They remind us of the custodial role of cultural places from one generation to the next; they tell of what engaged people at an earlier time and of the connection between our lifestyle, our health, the food we eat, the clothes we wear and the scientific discoveries of the past.

On a visit to London's Kew Gardens a friend took me to a small museum filled with an extraordinary collection of oil paintings. Inside a simple red-brick building is housed the work of the nineteenth-century English artist Marianne North. Like a temple for worshipping the bounty of nature, it's a wonderful complement to a trip to Kew Gardens. Marianne North built and paid for the gallery, to provide an artists' residency in the gardens. She stayed there herself and her work of 832 botanical paintings wallpaper the interior.

Marianne North visited Australia at the suggestion of Charles Darwin, who told her that her collection of botanical paintings was incomplete without a visit to Australia. An unmarried woman of independence, an artist and an adventurous traveller in the model of Lady Franklin, she was well connected in London society, where she mixed with leading intellectuals, all men, whom she took as role models. Through her paintings she recorded the journeys she made, to every continent, between 1871 and 1885. Although she is not acknowledged as a great artist, her paintings are like Instagram today, in that they're 'snapshots' of the places she visited and the strange flowers and animals she encountered. She had a scientific interest in recording unusual flora and flora from across the world and was keen to share her discoveries with like-minded others. She did this by donating a gallery, where she hung her paintings, which she had backed and numbered herself. She also painted the ornate doorways of the small temple – the gallery – to her work with garlands of flowers on a gilded background. Entering the gallery is like stepping into a jewel box from another time filled with brightly coloured fruit, birds and flowers – her paintings. En masse they are breathtaking; they capture time and reflect her preoccupation with scientific discovery and her sense of excitement with her discoveries. With this small museum, with its gilded and stencilled interior and its upper gallery, from which visitors can still share the world she captured with paint, she gifted a view of a world far away from Kew that included scenes of nature from the Americas, Asia and Australia, in a time when many would never leave London.

Marianne North lived in that time when educated women were seeking knowledge of the world around them. In creating her small museum Marianne was undoubtedly hoping to establish her reputation as an artist, but more than that she wanted to contribute to public education and learning and to enable other artists to study and paint the plant life she loved.

As well as the natural world, Marianne North was interested in cities and civilisation. When she arrived in Australia in 1879 she visited Brisbane, Sydney, Melbourne, Hobart and Perth. Of the Australian landscapes, she loved Western Australia most of all, which she described it as 'a natural flower garden'. Her opinion of Brisbane however was less complimentary, its being:

> most unattractive, a sort of overgrown village, with wide empty streets full of driving dust and sand, surrounded by wretched suburbs of wooden huts scattered over steep bare hills.

Sydney didn't fare much better, with her merely commenting: 'I didn't care for the town'. Of Melbourne she wrote:

> Melbourne is a noble city, and its gardens more beautiful than those of Sydney, with greater variety of ground, and lovely views over the river. It is by far the most real city in Australia, and the streets are as full of quickly moving people as those of London.

Her real interest in Australia lay in its animals and botanical life. Although she didn't visit Adelaide, had they lived at the same time she would have been the kind of visitor that Lady Ursula Hayward would have welcomed to her grand house, Carrick Hill.

Born as Ursula Barr Smith and grand-daughter of the wealthy Australian pastoralist, Thomas Barr Smith, the founder with Thomas Elder of the wool-broking firm of Elder Smith & Co., Carrick Hill was her home. Ursula married Bill Hayward, from the mercantile family that owned John Martins, once Adelaide's leading department store. Nestled in the foothills of Adelaide, Carrick Hill, with the beautiful gardens designed by her, is now open as a living museum for others to enjoy – her house, her art collection and the life she lived in 1930s Adelaide. When it was created, the house was designed to be the latest in style and modernity. Carrick Hill can easily be imagined as a house that hosted many a party; it is still used for weddings and parties, with the lawns and gardens often the setting for weddings. Carrick Hill was bequeathed by the Haywards to the people of South Australia.

The Friends of Carrick Hill, in their book *Carrick Hill: Heydays of the Haywards 1940–1970*, tell its story and list some of the famous visitors to the house. The actors who came to parties at Carrick Hill included the great names of screen and stage of the twentieth century. By the 1960s it had become a place where the artists, musicians and actors who visited the early Adelaide arts festivals would gather to party on the lawns walled by towering hedges and cooled at night by the soft summer gully winds.

A visit to a retrospective exhibition of the late Adelaide-born Australian artist Jeffrey Smart gave a special insight into the woman who created Carrick Hill. Ursula Hayward would have been pleased to see her house full of school children and art lovers, enjoying the work of Smart. She always had great confidence in Smart and supported him before he became an international success. In the exhibition was a postcard to 'Dear Ursula' sent by the young artist from New York, with all the excitement that a nineteen-year-old boy and artist from Adelaide would have felt arriving in New York. He was out in the world and on the road to success – and sharing it with his patron. Perhaps she bought his ticket? Those who knew Ursula Hayward said she was always generous and without pretention. When Edward Hayward received a knighthood and she became Lady Hayward, Jeffrey Smart is quoted as saying when Ursula was asked how she felt about being Lady Hayward. She replied: 'I'd rather have the measles'.

Carrick Hill is a little like the Isabella Stewart Gardner Museum in Boston, built as a kind of folly seeking a link to a more refined European past. Isabella Gardner, Mrs Jack, as she was known, brought architectural details from a Venetian Palazzo to make a grand entrance to her house in the Fenway, a quite different neighbourhood from the elegant city streets of Boston. Carrick Hill, built in the style of an English manor house, was built on the edge of the city in the foothills in the spirit of an Italian villa in the Florentine hills. Carrick Hill reflected the tradition of the wealthy Americans who liked to recreate European houses in Manhattan or Hollywood and shows the fashion and style of the era, a time when their wealthy owners were served breakfast on a tray after a party.

These women led privileged lives and yet they had a willingness to introduce new ideas and art into their worlds. Like Isabella Stewart Gardner, whose house was built earlier – in 1905 – and contained one of the first telephone lines, Ursula Hayward was a collector and lover of art, furniture and the decorative arts, and moved with the times. She had a telephone room, a flower room with a door to the garden, where she loved to arrange the flowers, a bathroom with heated towel rails, and one of Adelaide's first showers in her en suite bathroom. While Isabella had Gobelin and Aubusson tapestries, Ursula Hayward had rare William Morris curtains, rugs and tapestries from the latest catalogues from Liberty of London and made tapestries and embroideries herself. Many pieces from her collection are now in the Art Gallery of South Australia decorative arts collection.

The threads in women's lives are intertwined. After being at Carrick Hill I visited a friend of my mother, now Susie Brennan, the widow of Ursula's nephew, Ian Hayward, at home in North Adelaide.

It was to talk with her about her friend, the Sydney philanthropist and art collector, the late Ann Lewis, about whose contribution to Australia's contemporary art collections I write later. Talking with Susie Brennan, I found myself staring at a wall in her kitchen on which hung four brightly coloured and freely painted abstract oil paintings, with dollops of paint making the petals of still life flowers. Admiring the paintings, I was told they were by Aunt Ursula – Ursula Hayward.

The painting I love most in the Isabella Gardner Museum in her home town of Boston is her portrait by the Swedish artist Anders Zorn, which hangs on a stair. Mrs Gardner, or Mrs Jack, as she was nicknamed locally, wears a white dress and is depicted as an expansive personality, with her arms stretched wide, a figure larger than life stepping out of Boston and into life in Venice. The world was her oyster.

Like the Gardner house at Fenway Court in Boston, with its doors and windows from a Venetian palazzo, the young newly-wed Haywards bought much of the sixteenth-, seventeenth- and eighteenth-century panelling, doors, staircases and windows for their house from the demolition sale of Beaudesert, a Tudor mansion in Staffordshire, in the English countryside. After it had been shipped to Adelaide they commissioned a family friend and Adelaide architect, James Irwin, to design a state of the art 1930s house in the foothills of the city. With the appearance of a seventeenth-century English manor house, it was to have a modern twist. The guidebooks explain: 'oak panelling and pewter light fittings happily blend with heated towel rails, en suite bathrooms and intercom systems'. Such innovation may have been occurring in Hollywood but it was rare in Australia at the time and even rarer in Adelaide. Ursula Hayward's home, like the home of Isabella Stewart Gardner, is a window into her fantasy world, which we can enjoy today. Both these houses are still wonderful to visit and you can't be in them without feeling the personality of the women who once lived there.

Like Margaret's Olley's room and Sunday Reed's Heide, and

sculptor and artist Margo Lewers's house and garden, now the Penrith Regional Gallery in western Sydney, these places tell you much about the women who loved and made them. Their fantasies, passions, dreams and spirit are there for us to discover and still enjoy. Their houses exemplify the lives of women who have followed and lived their dreams.

Sunday Reed and her husband John Reed both came from wealthy Melbourne families and made a garden eighty years ago that has become one of Melbourne's most popular weekend visiting places. In the 1930s, young and just returned from Europe, the couple wanted to create a place for art and culture to flourish in Australia. They more than succeeded: today their former house and garden is an extensive sculpture garden, with their subsequent 1960s house converted to a gallery. A new exhibition space and café has been added to create a contemporary cultural museum in a spectacular landscape. While the young Reeds of Melbourne had less mannered plans, theirs were no less grand than the Haywards in Adelaide.

Enjoying Sunday's house and garden and viewing her collections, the visitor has a sense of what she believed in and the culture she was attempting to establish in Australia. Her lively and creative spirit is palpable. The heart garden still remains in the lawn at the side of the weatherboard house where the dream of Heide began. An interesting and enlightening place to visit because of its connection to the art world of the first half of the twentieth century, Heide also shows how life was lived with creativity at its heart. Sunday's famous open house attracted the leading members of Melbourne's art world and importantly led the way in support and love for the arts and the development of a philanthropic culture, which still today enriches the cultural life of Melbourne's inhabitants.

On a bright spring day, the visitor wandering through the gardens will encounter children playing, running and hiding in the twist and turns of Sunday's plantings. An art room hosts a Sunday morning art class for small boys and girls. Walking the paths of the walled garden feels as if we have entered a world for private lovers.

The world Sunday Reed created to share with her friends and lovers is now a place for everyone.

In 1935 the Reeds embarked on a bohemian way of life and they invited their friends to share it. Sunday was seen as a life-loving free spirit. Unable to have children, she filled her home with creative friends. She was an early and generous patron to many of Australia's greatest artists, including Sidney Nolan and Joy Hester, who spent time at the first Heide weatherboard farmhouse. The museum claims that some of Nolan's famous Ned Kelly paintings were painted in the simple dining room there. Heide was Sunday Reed's inspiration, a way of Australian life that was cultured, healthy and free, and she invited Australians to share it. She was health-conscious and believed in the benefits of home-grown food and in simple Mediterranean provincial food, which did not become mainstream in Australia till decades later.

The kitchen garden at Heide still bursts with abundance – spinach, broad beans, rhubarb, kale, peas and sweet peas – and a profusion of roses and the perennials of a Monet-like flower garden. Bright-blue cornflowers tangled with thyme; blue borage flowers beneath a mass of roses – of deep blood-reds, flaming oranges and tumbling yellows – all rambling together over red brick walls and taking over the paths in the garden. Lettuces, iris and roses mingle against an unlikely backdrop of native gums. The old walled gardens are lush and beckon like a secret garden inviting us into a better world.

The sculpture park, the two houses, both now museums, and the cafés and galleries are a magnificent experience, enabling people of all ages to escape to a place that is both a green and quiet haven and an exciting and stimulating cultural experience in the suburbs, away from the inner-urban grey of Melbourne. Heide, which embodies the life of art and ideas Sunday Reed embraced, has become a rich cultural site and an important contemporary art museum. At that time artists and intellectuals were attracted to the idealised country life, away from the suburban life that mainstream Australia was embracing. Heide was an escape from the speed of the post-war city and where artists and intellectuals would gather and where music, art and ideas could flower. A visit to Heide still invites us to step into a world of ideas and beauty, though now the houses and garden are no longer surrounded by farmland but circled by a highway, suburbs and streets.

Making a garden was important to Sunday Reed, with her kitchen garden one of the first to be designed and planted with vegetables, herbs and fruit not found in Australian gardens at the time. Sunday Reed was ahead of her time, a creator of her own lifestyle movement, one that pioneered a freer, relaxed and healthy Australian outdoor life, where growing and cooking organic food was central to wellbeing and happiness. Beyond the kitchen garden a scented ornamental garden, reminiscent of Europe, with a tunnel of roses and violets and hedges of lavender was planted; beyond that again the Yarra River and the Australian bush. The house was host to a who's who of Australian artists and their wives and lovers. The Boyds, Percivals, Nolans, Albert Tucker and Joy Hester and Danila Vasilieff and Georges and Mirka Mora were all part of the circle who came and stayed and shared in the daily life, the work in the garden, the library and the conversation at Heide. But that is another story.

Sunday and John Reed commissioned the modernist house in which they lived until the final year of their lives. Now the Heide Museum, it was designed by the Melbourne architect, David McGlashen, in 1967. Known as Heide II, it was to become Australia's first contemporary art house museum. Again Sunday Reed led a fashion for modernist houses and furniture. She and John Reed both died in 1981, just weeks after the house had opened as Heide Park and Art Gallery, with most of their collection remaining in the house. In 2006 the landscape architect Elizabeth Peck oversaw major additions to the landscape. Heide has become one of Melbourne's and Australia's most important cultural places.

In Sydney it was Margo Lewers and her husband Gerald who gathered artists and bohemians into their house and garden at Emu Plains on the banks of the Nepean River at Penrith. At the time their house was like Heide, in the country, miles from the established suburbs of Sydney. The idea behind a house in the country was that it would also leave behind the strict codes of suburban life.

Tanya Crothers and Darani Lewers, Margo Lewers's two daughters, grew up in the old stone house in Penrith, white-washed to appear modern, with its rambling garden of ponds and sculptured delight. Tanya Crothers told me that her parents created the garden with a team of friends as willing labourers on weekends. The architect, Lawrence Nield, was one of the children whose parents were friends of the Lewers. He remembers regular working bees and long lunches at the house at Emu Plains, which was a rare haven for like-minded bohemian souls – architects and artists and their freewheeling children. It was a house, like Heide, where the woman was at the centre: Margo Lewers was supported by her husband in putting into practice her commitment to the creation of a 'total environment'. Her art works, his garden sculptures, the interior design of the house with its modern kitchen and 'Danish design school' furniture, the then avant garde architecture of a glass-walled living room off the kitchen, which opened to the walled back garden, were all new to Australian life. All this created the possibility of a more relaxed and open way of living. Tanya Crothers, also an artist, explains that the house and garden were created as a demonstration of how her mother believed that every aspect of daily life could be designed and integrated, from the presentation of food, to bathroom mosaics, and structures such as drain pipes.

Through her house and work Margo Lewers is now recognised as a significant influence on the way modernism was introduced to Sydney. In the 1930s Lewers opened the Notanda Gallery, the first interior design shop in Sydney to embrace modernist principles, designing and selling furniture, pottery and fabrics. Although the shop only lasted a short time – until the outbreak of the Second World War – it was a woman who had prepared the path for the acceptance of the work of the women artists and the male architects, such as Harry Seidler, Neville Gruzman and other contemporary designers, the modernists whose work was first seen as truly radical and anarchic by comparison with the Victorian and Edwardian housing and Californian Bungalow style that had preceded it.

Margo Lewers, wife, mother and artist, was an activist for design. As one of the initiators and the Secretary of Sydney's Contemporary Art Society, which was established in 1941, she changed perceptions of art and what it is. Later she worked with recently arrived refugees, introducing the public to new ideas from Europe. She also organised an exhibition of a collection of paintings brought to Australia by European refugees, giving local art lovers a first-hand experience of many of the twentieth century's modernist masters.

Visiting the garden on a hot Sunday morning reminded me of the stone houses of my childhood in Adelaide, many of which were later 'modernised' with the addition of a sunroom on the back and a walled garden. But that happened in Adelaide in the 1960s and this was two decades earlier.

Now the Penrith Regional Gallery, the Lewers house remains the mecca for lovers of art and food, just as it was when Margo Lewers lived there. The garden is still there, but has links to a café extension on the side of the house and a contemporary gallery space. The house, with its wonderful full-length French windows and its bright stained glass around the front door, sits happily in the garden, white-washed in and out and providing a perfect gallery space for the work of the young people being displayed on the day of my visit. Curator Anne Loxley was one of its first directors: a leader in creating contemporary art for local communities. Margo Lewers would surely have approved of Anne Loxley being in charge.

Inspired by a visit to the Butchart Gardens in Vancouver, Sydney philanthropists Bill and Imelda Roche created a stunning private garden in the Hunter Valley outside Sydney. Nestled at the foothills of the Brokenback Ranges, in the heart of the Hunter vineyards, the magnificent Hunter Valley Gardens cover twenty-five hectares, containing sunken gardens, oriental gardens, rose gardens, water gardens set with sensational vistas and colours, scents, and walking paths extending for eight kilometres. Although their garden was designed as a private garden as a retirement project, Bill and Imelda Roche have given the community the garden in the tradition of the Reeds and the Haywards, but in this instance as a pleasure ground for families and children.

These women, collectors and keepers of things they found precious, liked to share their homes, gardens and treasures and how they lived. They wanted to share their lives. Their houses and gardens show us the different kinds of places that women make, at first not intended for the public, but later shared through the generous spirit of the women who created them.

JUDITH NIELSEN, *collector, philanthropist and founder of Sydney's contemporary art space White Rabbit Gallery.*

WOMEN'S GIFTS

The arts are what we stay alive for, what we work for all week, what we dream about, what connects us and indeed, what some will say makes us human.

CATE BLANCHETT

In the urban life we live, with its extremes of wealth and poverty, it is important for everyone to have access to art and creativity; these help us to make sense of life and to give our lives meaning. Art shows us beauty or it surprises us, it assists us to process our joys and sorrows, it is a way to keep in touch with ourselves, a way to process thoughts and to be in touch with our own feelings. We need this in our frantic urban lives.

Our cities and communities need places that invite people into a world of ideas beyond an escapist trip to the movies, although we still need that escape. Cities are much more than collections of buildings; they are places where people gather for art, culture and commerce. Cultural places are places we often visit alone but where we don't feel alone. We share what we see and experience with others, and we feel a sense of belonging and connection, even if we don't know or don't talk to the others participating in the cultural event. Cultural places fulfil a need to gather, to share, to learn and to experience something unexpected, or beautiful, or challenging.

Culture can nurture us, and the women who give us cultural places to share art and ideas change the lives of others. There is vitality and generosity in sharing a private artistic life in a public way. In Sydney, two women, Gene Sherman and Judith Neilson, have both established galleries as public cultural institutions. They are motivated to share their interests, their artistic journeys and discoveries, their ideas and those of others by providing exhibitions and places for artists to exhibit, and audiences to gather and share. Each of these generous women has done this in her own distinctive way. Both are collectors of contemporary art who invite the community to be part of their visual world and to explore contemporary culture. The work of both involves their families and spans two generations.

Gene Sherman is the creative force behind the Sherman Cultural Arts Foundation (SCAF), a foundation with long threads reaching into Sydney's artistic life and funded jointly with her husband. Each year the foundation runs a series of exhibitions in the Paddington art space that was once the Sherman Gallery, a space where many leading contemporary artists were first shown and applauded for their work. Gene Sherman loves conversation and discussions with the artists, visiting intellectuals and with the audience. She has supported the publication of books and new writing and new design and architecture. Gene, supported by her husband Brian, has a generous spirit. For years she opened her home for the opening night parties for her artists. These expansive dinners in the family's Paddington terrace house were nights to remember, with people perched in every corner of the house engrossed in conversation, surrounded by the fabulous Sherman art collection. It was a place that new friends, deals and even marriages were made.

Gene Sherman always seems to be smiling and always interested in people and their creative lives. She is forthright and compassionate; after a childhood in South Africa, the freedom and opportunity of her adult life in Sydney has seen her embedded into the city's cultural life as a gallery owner and philanthropist. Gene believes women have always been a huge influence on the support given to the arts in Australia, but often in the quiet role of being the 'significant other'. At SCAF Gene Sherman is 'hands on'. As a young grandmother and always stylish in black couture clothes, she takes an active role in driving the artistic program. She is focused on supporting the next generation of artists and art lovers and on teaching and exchanging ideas through culture.

Gene Sherman's face beams when she talks of having children from the local area in the gallery working with artists and making art and food and major installations at the SCAF gallery and studio space. She says there is more demand than can be met. 'Most of the major public galleries have programs for children but they add them as an afterthought with a tiny budget.' She makes the point that Brisbane's Gallery of Modern Art is the exception, in that it has commissioned and acquired contemporary works for children, which makes the organisation a leader in children's arts programs in Australia. Similarly at SCAF, when planning the artistic program, children are not an afterthought as an audience.

Seeing Gene Sherman in action unlocking art for the children is a bit like watching the magic of a modern-day Mary Poppins. Explaining the artwork surrounding them to a group of utterly attentive five to eight-year-olds, she tells them that children in the Philippines live in houses similar to the cardboard-house installation, *In-Habit Project Another Country*, by a husband-and-wife team, Alfredo Juan Aquilizan and Isabel Gaudinez-Aquilizan. It is a remarkable installation and fills the space in the gallery from floor to ceiling, clinging organically to scaffolding, reminding us of the real stilted houses built by the poor fishing communities north of Australia who have no land to call their own. The project is not specifically aimed at children, but Gene Sherman, with her skills as a former teacher, has the little ones asking questions about water and power and storms and how these people live. Then the children go off to use the recycled cardboard to make their own 'house' to add to the work.

Gene Sherman's philosophy is not to talk down to children but to invite them into the adult world of contemporary art and to expand their world in the process. The Junior Art Forum @ SCAF is contemporary art for contemporary kids and involves children working with an artist and making installations, which are then exhibited for the pleasure of anyone who wanders into the Paddington gallery. Like Marianne North once did at Kew, the Shermans have long provided an artist's cottage opposite the gallery as temporary home for visiting artists in residence. In a motherly way Gene Sherman has made SCAF an independent oasis to nurture artists, audiences, design and ideas.

The delightful White Rabbit Gallery quickly found its place on the contemporary art lover's map of Sydney when it opened in 2009. Judith Neilson, its founder, is a collector of contemporary Chinese art. She opened the gallery in a converted warehouse, which was once a Rolls Royce repair shop in the constantly evolving inner-city suburb of Chippendale. Once home to workers and warehouses, Chippendale still has a few workshops, warehouses and studios, but it is now home to urban hipsters, students and artists and those who have always lived there in narrow terrace houses. White Rabbit is a mother-and-daughter project driven by Judith and her daughter, Paris. The creative direction is theirs and the program of exhibitions is entirely privately funded, enabling complete independence in what is shown. They influence every aspect of the way the gallery is programmed and designed. With its small scale and focus, it has a relaxed and quite different feel from a public cultural institution – from the moment you step into the tea house with its birdcages swinging from the rafters.

Judith Neilson, an art school graduate in graphic art and textiles, describes herself as an artist and an appreciator of art. The idea behind White Rabbit was to open a not-for-profit gallery, which would be open to the public at no charge. The gallery generally shows two exhibitions a year, and is a place to show works from Judith Neilson's private collection. Like Gene Sherman's SCAF, White Rabbit is also a place of ideas. Talks are hosted, reading groups meet there, books are launched, although the aim of encouraging an understanding of the work and culture of contemporary China and celebrating talented artists remains central.

Neilson reminds me of a latter-day explorer, similar to those eighteenth- and nineteenth-century women who travelled to new worlds searching for the new and undiscovered. Like Marianne North and Lady Franklin, she is a cultural explorer wanting to share and make sense of what she finds in China today. Her establishment of the White Rabbit Gallery enables her to share a world she has discovered, one that not everybody has the opportunity to visit and experience first-hand.

China is a huge cultural force for Australians in the early years of the twenty-first century. Our economies are linked and the contemporary culture of that country is something young Australians want to engage with and understand. In ways that are fun, surprising and often challenging, White Rabbit Gallery encourages this to happen, making it an important place in the cultural landscape of Australia. It reflects Australia's current cultural interests and our need to make sense of our place in Asia and in the culture of the most dominant Asian nation. The name 'White Rabbit' suggests that it's a surprising and fun place to visit. It is a place given generously by a woman, and it has become her passion and that of her daughter and a gift to people she may never meet.

In the Adelaide Hills the philanthropist and a lover of music and art, Ulrike Klein, began what is now the international Jurlique cosmetics and skincare company. Having settled in Adelaide with her husband, Ulrike began growing the herbs that in Germany and Switzerland are used as the base of so many health and beauty products. From these small plants a beauty empire grew, which was subsequently sold to major investors and is now an international brand. Ngeringa Farm, where it all began, is still hidden away in a green valley beyond the Adelaide Hills town of Mt Barker. Here the landscape unfolds like a series of painterly scenes by the South Australian landscape artist, Sir Hans Heysen – golden yellow in the summer dry, and green as Ireland in the winter and spring, with majestic gums punctuating the paddocks where sheep graze. The farm now has a family vineyard rolling down the hill towards the sun. A wonderful sculpture garden, a performance and exhibition space make a new locale for enjoying art, food, wine and music. Ulrike Klein owns a priceless collection of instruments made in the seventeenth century by Guadagnini in

Cremona, the northern Italian town where Stradivarius had his workshop. She adores chamber music and has made it her mission to support it. She knows that the best way to support young Australian musicians is to provide fine instruments and opportunities for audiences to hear them play.

These rare sweet-toned instruments, a viola, violin and cello, are lent to talented Australian musicians. Now Ulrike is making sure her foundation will always support chamber music, particularly that played by young musicians, by providing a purpose-built concert space through her Klein Family Foundation. The Ngeringa Farm Music and Arts Centre, set amongst lines of vines in the rolling hills outside Adelaide, will have a sculpture garden designed by artist Winnie Pelz, a woman who has always been involved in Adelaide's rich cultural life. The arts centre project was delivered under the guidance of Foundation Manager Alison Beare. This little heaven in the Adelaide Hills will was created and shared through women working together to make a place for others to enjoy what they love.

Philanthropic women have always been quietly present in Australia. Perth's Janet Holmes à Court is a well-known Australian who, for decades, has supported the performing arts, culture and architecture. An early collector of Western Australian Indigenous artists such as Rover Thomas, she supported Aboriginal artists by buying their work and encouraging others to take it seriously as art. Her Leeuwin Estate winery has a gallery and exhibition space, showing just a few paintings from her astounding collection, and is used widely for many kinds of cultural events. She has long supported Australia's pavilion in Venice the art and architecture Biennales. Some women, such as the widowed Janet Holmes à Court, have had their own money to gift, while others have used their husbands' wealth for their acts of generosity. In Australian cities, places that offer insights into other cultures can do more than add to city life, they can encourage harmony and link people of diverse cultures and different faiths. What is made less foreign and strange helps to cultivate understanding, connection and the elimination of race-based prejudice. Sharing stories, art, music and food, even without speaking the same language, builds understanding.

A woman who loved Asian art and gave to Australian cultural life is the late Yasuko Myer, wife of the late Ken Myer, eldest son of Sidney and Merlyn Myer. She was beautiful, and from Japan. She and her husband, once head of the Melbourne retail dynasty and well known as Chairman of the ABC, donated two significant collections of Japanese art to the Art Gallery of New South Wales in Sydney and the Queensland Art Gallery in Brisbane. Both husband and wife were tragically killed in a plane crash, but are remembered for their gift of Asian art and beginning an awareness of Asia that is now mainstream and important in Australian public art collections. The collections, as well as being objects of beauty, reflect an interest in our region. People in the museum world say that Yasuko Myer's support for projects like the Asian Arts Triennial at the Queensland Art Gallery encouraged a new engagement with the ideas and cultures of neighbouring countries.

In Sydney, Goldie Sternberg, who with her husband Ed amassed a significant collection of Chinese art, gave this to the Asian Wing of the Art Gallery of New South Wales. Inspired by London's legendary Serpentine Pavilion project in Kensington Gardens, philanthropist Naomi Milgram has given Melbourne MPavilion. This annual architectural commission with its free program of design-related events set in the Queen Victoria Gardens is advancing the importance of design in our life. In these public cultural places ideas and opinions can be shared and exchanged; these are the safe zones needed to air new and sometimes contentious ideas in our cities.

Melbourne's Federation Square was being planned during the years preceding Australia's Centenary as a nation. The building design attracted controversy and there was some uncertainty about how readily a new public place would be adopted as a kind of cultural hub by the people of Melbourne. Its aim was to be a great gathering place, a place for cultural activities and where ideas could be heard. Across the road from the grand Victoriana of Flinders Street Station and the soaring St Paul's Cathedral spires, the series of linked geometric glass cubes proposed for an extension to the National Gallery of Victoria and for community uses raised conservative eyebrows. No one was quite sure whether the grand Centenary of Federation project, to open in 2001, would be Melbourne's white elephant or if the place would work. But work it has, very soon after its completion becoming an important public space, the place where people gather for protest, celebration or sorrow. This happened under the guiding hand of its CEO, Kate Brennan. Ensuring that Federation Square became a success story was seen as a challenge: it had to work financially, but much more importantly, a sense of ownership amongst the people of Melbourne for Federation Square as a place for public gathering needed to be nurtured. It is now a special place in the life of that city and its people. The outdoor plaza opposite the station has been a place to cheer, mourn and farewell, to say sorry, to watch the grand final, to see the Queen, to enjoy a rock concert and a place just to meet friends. Kate Brennan agrees it could have gone either way, but her key focus was on being sensitive to the life of the community:

> When the community comes up with a good idea, supporting it and allowing it to happen is really important, whether it is as a gathering place for a protest or to celebrate the grand final. It needed to be a place of relevance.

Federation Square seems to have found its role in the city. In its first ten years Federation Square received eighty million visitors. Almost ninety per cent of the events at Federation Square are free public events. The BMW Edge in Federation Square is a performance space used by many of Melbourne's artistic community, including the writers' festival and chamber concerts, while the wide brick plaza has become an adaptable stage for community life to play out and for people to explore ideas as a community.

Food, film, music, knitting, books, zumba and salsa dancing, and sport all take place here, tapping into what the urban community of Melbourne is looking for on weekends. Federation Square is a public place on a grand scale and in a grand city, but it works as much more than a well-designed building made of bricks, glass and mortar. It is lively, vibrant and welcoming. As the New York Vice President of Projects for Public Spaces said:

> Federation Square is one of the boldest and most successful public spaces in the world. The Melbourne community has gone further than any city in recent history in realizing the potential for a central square to serve as a major civic and cultural destination. Bringing the square to life every day, the innovative and responsive management and programming of the square are performed at a level that raises the bar.

Melbourne is the first Australian city to have a permanent circus home, thanks to the planning and advocacy of two determined women and some generous men. Australia's Circus Oz, an animal-free circus had a long-held dream of a permanent home. Australia has had an enduring tradition – from the 1800s – of circus performance, with the annual arrival of the big tent and troopers in big country towns and cities highly anticipated. Circus Oz's Chair, Wendy McCarthy, and its founding manager, Linda Mickleborough, persuaded the Victorian Government to redevelop the old Collingwood TAFE site and, in the best traditions of the company, the Circus Oz manager, Lou Oppenheim, saw it delivered. Together, three women made this happen. Cities are fluid and places happen when communities need them and inspired leadership responds to needs. Circus Oz promotes the best of the Australian spirit: generosity, diversity, death-defying bravery and a fair go for all. The transformation of Circus Oz into a company that tours Australia, and even performs in New York, reflects a change in urban culture, which was recognised by these women, who decided to take a long view for their community and for the circus artists, ensuring the gift of a permanent home.

Linda Mickleborough and Kate Brennan resemble many of the women who have worked for decades in the space where the arts meet community life, nurturing art by creating public places where everyone can enjoy the arts. Scottish-born Elizabeth Ann Macgregor, OBE, has dedicated her life in Sydney to making the Museum of Contemporary Art (MCA) a great place for people of all ages and walks of life to meet and discover contemporary art and new ideas. To the shock of her friends in the London contemporary art scene, she chose to make her career in Sydney, arriving in 1999 to run the Museum of Contemporary Art and becoming a force in building the audience for contemporary art in Australia. The tartan she once wore boldly has become subtle, but there is nothing subtle about the reach of her presence in the Australian contemporary arts scene. The MCA, which she has nurtured, might never have been there but for the diligence, persistence and curatorial vision of the partnership between Bernice Murphy and Leon Paroissien, who were its foundation artistic directors. Since the battle for its establishment in Sydney, the MCA has extended its reach and under Elizabeth Ann Macgregor's direction the museum presents art that is sometimes fun, sometimes puzzling, playful, startling and challenging, but it is available to everyone and not merely to the cultural elite. As CEO of the Museum of Contemporary Art, she has been an indefatigable and successful fundraiser. An article published in *Crikey* tells of her success.

> When the flame-haired Scotswoman took over in 1999, the MCA was in crisis – starved of cash, widely perceived as elitist and suffering in a sandstone building too small to house a permanent collection. Since Macgregor took over, visitor numbers have sky-rocketed, corporate sponsorships have increased and the gallery now has 50% more floor space thanks to the new Mordant Wing, designed in the shape of a stack of cubes.

In 1999 Elizabeth Ann went to war with the Lord Mayor of the day, Frank Sartor, to prevent the demolition of the 1930s maritime building in which the MCA was housed. The demolition would have closed the museum that had first been established as a public institution with works from the University of Sydney's Power collection. Later as Minister for the Arts in New South Wales, Frank Sartor made peace and promised funding for its expansion. At the time of the threatened demolition Elizabeth Ann argued that:

> It was not a building that should be knocked down and rebuilt. I did what I felt was right for the museum. It was not a time to think about how do we put up a glamorous new building.

She still sees the MCA with its new spaces not as a building but as a place for people. 'A museum is a place for connection', she explains. Elizabeth Ann's focus has always been on connecting art with audiences. As a twenty-year-old she travelled around Scotland in a truck taking art to remote communities decades before the term 'pop-up art' was coined. Keeping the museum admission free meant increasing the numbers of visitors by creating an artistic program that drew crowds, which in turn meant that the museum activity outgrew the space in the building. Elizabeth Ann took on the challenge of expansion, and its program now expands beyond the MCA's walls, to the growing community of western Sydney.

Elizabeth Ann Macgregor explains that there is a woman's story behind both the collection and the expansion of the museum. Two women collectors, Lotte Smorgan from Melbourne and Ann Lewis from Sydney, were both catalysts in the development of the museum. Both gave major parts of their personal collections to the museum. Ann Lewis, a twentieth-century pioneer of contemporary art in Australia with her experimental Sydney Gallery A, was a warm, larger-than-life girl from the bush when she discovered contemporary art in New York. One of her lifelong friends, Susie Brennan, a member of Adelaide's Hayward family, says Ann Lewis was always there for her friends in times of trouble and always gave to the communities she was part of. They met in 1958 and became friends immediately. Ann stayed with her friend for Adelaide's legendary first Festival of Arts, where parties stretched into the night under the cool vines of Decca's Place restaurant as the cultural crowds gathered to hear the dazzling Russian poet Yevtushenko read his work – and enjoy the wine that flows in Adelaide.

Susie Brennan describes Ann Lewis as a countrywoman who 'gave and gave with a generosity of spirit that should be bottled'. Dining at Ann Lewis's house in the harbourside suburb of Vaucluse was relaxed, yet memorable, for anyone invited. It was lunch or dinner in a jewel box of a room: glazed emerald green walls with a painting on the ceiling – *Five Bells* after Kenneth Slessor's poem, painted in 1964 by the Australian artist John Olsen. Laughter, wine, serious conversation and good food and you felt you were in Oz's emerald city. Beyond, the garden meandered down to the harbour below and views of sparkling water stretched across Rose Bay to Point Piper. A modest house from the street although reminiscent of a small French Riviera villa, it was not fussy or over-decorated like many of its neighbours, just filled with amazing paintings and sculpture, life and laughter.

The catalogue of the fifty-four works from her collection given by her to the MCA describes her as 'one of the most admired and respected members of the Australian and indeed international art world, dedicated to art, to supporting artists and art institutions'. Ann Lewis gave to Sydney's MCA, the National Gallery of Australia, the Newcastle Regional Gallery and the Regional Gallery in Moree, in western New South Wales, where she grew up. It was Ann Lewis who made the first major private gift for the latest expansion of the museum. And yet Elizabeth Ann Macgregor says she had to persuade Ann Lewis to allow her to name the Lewis Library at the MCA after her. Ann Lewis, in common with many women who have given generously, never sought celebrity status.

Lewis was a pioneer in contemporary art in Australia. She was a board member of the National Gallery of Australia and twice commissioner for the Australian Pavilion at the Venice Biennale and from 1972 a member of the International Council of the Museum of Modern Art in New York, becoming its vice president in 1993. Artists were at home in her houses, including in her New York loft apartment, where Australian curators and artists often stayed.

Elizabeth Ann Macgregor explains that Catriona Mordant is another woman who, with her husband Simon, helped to make the expansion possible by giving and encouraging gifts from others. The persistence of women in supporting the MCA's expansion has meant that a new generation of visitors to the museum enjoys its riches. The expansion has added places like the rooftop outdoor plaza, named after the philanthropist Lotte Smorgan, which is full on most days and offers an affordable lunch and some of the best views of the Bridge and the harbour. When Sydney's winter light show *Vivid* projects art onto the building, MCA Artbar attracts a young crowd. They have a free run of the building to enjoy the collection and the installations curated by leading artists. This is like an opening night party for young patrons. MCA curator Anne Loxley says 'the new spaces invite everybody in, not just the opening night elites'.

Like Elizabeth Ann Macgregor, Lynda Dorrington in Perth has been a force for contemporary culture and design in her city. Linda as CEO of FORM, an institution focused on the value of design, is credited by insiders with putting Perth's cultural life on the agenda and for making the city richer and more exciting for its community. Her voice engaged business and enticed government and private investment into the city's cultural life and places at the time of the last mining boom. As a voice for community and culture, she has influenced the creation of city places for people's enjoyment of the arts by encouraging investment in theatres, cultural places and a rethinking of the city's heart. In 2013, this complex work in city-making was recognised when she was awarded the Dame Elisabeth Murdoch Arts Leadership Award from the Australia Council for the Arts for 'demonstrating vision, commercial acumen and strategic thinking in engagement with business and by encouraging increased giving to the arts'.

Women work in their different ways. There has been a long tradition of philanthropy by women to cultural places and places of learning, including libraries, and this continues across generations in different ways. Dame Elisabeth Murdoch gave generously to make new spaces at the State Library of Victoria and was a major donor to the State Library of South Australia. Patricia Michell, an Adelaide philanthropist, has taken South Australia's State Library under her generous wing as a donor and chair of its Foundation.

Sydney's Customs House Library at Circular Quay is one of the most outstanding achievements of the urbanist and philanthropist, Lucy Turnbull. Many of the women whose work I have discussed were at first modest about their achievements; Lucy was no exception in not wishing to claim the making of the library as her achievement. Before being the first woman Lord Mayor of Sydney, Lucy Turnbull, served on the Council of Lord Mayor Sartor. The city's Director of Design, Bridget Smyth, who worked with Lucy at the time says: 'It was Lucy's idea and the idea would never have got through the political maze without her focus, skill and determination'. It seems she was ahead of a trend in reinventing libraries as important places for urban life. Today libraries are vital wifi hubs and meeting places for urban communities. The Customs House is now a library, a programmed exhibition space and a place for talks and community meetings. Lucy Turnbull explained to me that: 'nobody really wanted to own the Customs House. It was a wonderful building but it didn't work commercially and even after Café Sydney was a success on the rooftop the ground floor was empty'.

Encouraging a rethink of a proposed design, which would have had escalators scissoring the grand foyer space, she envisioned it as a library and as the great public place for books and ideas that it has become. Sydney's Customs House, accessible by train and ferry and near the historic Rocks precinct, is the perfect location for a public use, especially as a library.

Lucy Turnbull drove the library project that may yet be Australia's first twenty-four-hour library.

> It has a strong emotional place in my heart. After it opened I wandered in one day and saw some small boys with superman capes zooming over the model of the city that sits under glass on the floor and it brought tears to my eyes.

The women who give understand that the education that libraries enable enriches people's lives. If there are no books and no peace to read at home – there is the refuge of a public library.

Until her death in 2012, aged 103, Dame Elisabeth Murdoch, the mother of media baron Rupert Murdoch, was perhaps Australia's leading arts and culture philanthropist. In addition to the recent expansion of the State Library of Victoria she contributed to a new chamber music recital hall in Melbourne, named after her. She also supported the care of important Aboriginal heritage and gave to music, the visual arts and other libraries. Her grandson once told me she gave much more than she was recognised for, quietly and privately supporting artists and their work.

Dame Merlyn Myer was another Melbourne woman with the insight and generosity to deliver a gift that would change the urban life of the city across generations. Born Margery Merlyn Baillieu, she married Sidney Myer, founder of the retail dynasty, with whom she had four children. In 1959 she was the catalyst, through the Sidney Myer Fund, for the Sidney Myer Music Bowl as a gift to the people of Victoria. The Bowl created a public place where millions have enjoyed performances in the park. This gift showed foresight: she could imagine the pleasure of gathering together with a crowd out of doors for Christmas carols, great symphonies, opera and rock music. This is a place where many would have heard their first choral, operatic or symphony performance, often free, under the southern stars. The Merlyn Theatre at Melbourne's Malthouse was named in her honour and acknowledges the support provided to the theatre through the Sidney Myer Fund. Even the Melbourne Symphony Orchestra came into being with a foundation grant from the Sidney Myer family to the University of Melbourne. Her daughter, Lady Marigold Southey, carried on the family tradition of giving. Another daughter, the late Neilma Gantner, founded a music festival at the coastal town of Bermagui in southern New South Wales, the Four Winds Festival. North of Melbourne, east of Canberra and south of Sydney, the Festival

DAME MERLYN MYER, *whose inspired idea was the gift of a music bowl for the people of Melbourne, a place where millions first heard a symphony or opera live on stage.*

will endure because of her endowment. She provided a chamber recital hall, called the Windsong Pavilion, which sits lightly on the land, above the Festival's open air sound shell.

In cities today arts and culture and corporate and political life are still closely intertwined, as they have always been. Corporate leaders chair arts boards and support the arts through giving time and through sponsorship. The czars of business and the arts rub shoulders with political leaders. Funding for the arts and culture from the public purse, despite the important function that community arts and high culture both play in city life, is never easy to gain. Women influence the giving of their husbands and partners and others give themselves. Maria Meyers, wife of the Melbourne Queen's Counsel, Alan Meyers, has given not only generous funding but also countless hours of her life to the many cultural causes she supports. The influence of women as donors, advocates, catalysts and supporters in making cultural places is vital to the life of our cities.

These are stories of women who have both influenced their husbands or have themselves given a great deal to generations of Australians towards the cultural places our cities need. They represent only a small number of the many stories that could be told. In museums, galleries, libraries, performances spaces and botanic gardens across Australia there are so many more women who volunteer time, giving their energy and expertise to help these places remain viable. Theirs is crucial work in Australia's community life as much as in its cultural life. It is especially important to celebrate the women who have boldly created the places in cities that enable new and sometimes challenging ideas to be seen and heard and which encourage the next generation to create places for their times. As people need more and more costly infrastructure for transport, health and education in our growing cities and as the public funds for the arts shrink, it is becoming more crucial for people to give ideas and beauty, time and dollars.

The American urbanist, Jane Jacobs, wrote: 'A city's wholeness in bringing together communities of interest is one of its assets, possibly the greatest'. Sport brings people together in great numbers in most Australian cities. Sport will always be part of our mainstream culture and there will always be places for sport to be played and watched. The cultural places in our cities that women have played such a substantial role in providing help to make us whole. Art and cultural places help us to make sense of who we are. Sometimes they give us beauty or challenge us, but always moments that allow us to escape from the intensity of urban life. We need inspiration, wonder and surprise from the places we visit and share. The women who have invested in sharing a world they have created and loved – from Dame Merlyn Myer to Gene Sherman – give a rare gift of ideas, hope and, often, just simple pleasure. As the feminist writer Jeanette Winterson says: 'Creativity is on the side of health. It isn't the thing that drives us mad. It is the capacity in us that tries to save us from madness'.

New places such as the White Rabbit Gallery, the Circus Oz Melba Spiegeltent, Sherman Contemporary Art Foundation, the Pavilion at Bermagui and Ngeringa Arts reflect a response to changing contemporary culture and community needs. Having access to places to enjoy cultural life is growing exponentially as more people live in cities. New places like those in this story will always be needed if our cities are to continue to reflect the changing culture of Australians. The activism, support, imagination and drive of generous women will continue to make new places for their communities.

CULTURAL BOULEVARDS

It is prudent to have patience.

DAME ROMA MITCHELL

Dame Roma Mitchell, who lived on Adelaide's North Terrace, loved it and all that it represented as a great cultural boulevard. As the first female governor of South Australia and of any Australian state, Dame Roma set a path to be followed by many women in Australia and not merely in her home town of Adelaide.

Dame Roma, who balanced the ability to be truly part of Adelaide's community life while holding its highest offices, had the distinction of being the first woman to be Chancellor of the University of Adelaide. She was also the first woman to be appointed a Supreme Court Judge, in 1965 in South Australia.

She was appointed governor of South Australia in 1991, moving to live on North Terrace at Government House. She cared about her city and with a gentle approach took up the cause of the renewal of Adelaide's grand cultural boulevard, North Terrace. It was the street where she lived, alongside the state parliament and the Adelaide Festival Centre. She loved to walk across the road to enjoy the theatre, concerts and opera. North Terrace is the street where she had walked as a young student to the University of Adelaide to read law, her great love. In her Government House home on North Terrace she held soirees, performances, poetry readings and recitals in support of the city's cultural life. She supported young artists making their

DAME ROMA MITCHELL, *watching over North Terrace.*

way in the tough world of the performing arts by inviting them to give concerts.

She and my grandmother were friends. I once took my grandmother, then in her nineties, to tea with her friend Roma. They were surprising friends, and in that vast house with its grand rooms we sat upstairs in the small simple sitting room where Dame Roma was most at home. They were women with a sense of fun and recognised in one another an energy and vitality at their core and the importance of giving, while maintaining a sense of the ridiculous in order to survive in life. They shared a refusal to see themselves as other than women in their prime, no matter their age, and both always made younger friends.

Dame Roma understood what North Terrace embodied for the people of Adelaide. Places are more than bricks and mortar. North Terrace is a street that has represented the achievements of the city's cultural life since settlement in 1836 and still does. It makes a connection to the past, while being a place for ideas, education, politics and change that looks to the future. Adelaide's North Terrace is unlike any other street in Australia, a grand city boulevard where Adelaide's cultural life brews. Remade in the past decade as an inviting public space, it is now a place to promenade, meet friends or sit in the sunshine or shade. It remains a place where Adelaide's power games, plotting and decision-making take place and it is home to the powerful men-only Adelaide Club and the more genteel but no less central women's club, the Queen Adelaide Club.

Adelaide's North Terrace was first imagined as a cultural boulevard by Colonel William Light, the city's planner. He visualised it as a boulevard with very public aspirations: it was to meet the educational and cultural needs of the people of the then young, independent colony of South Australia. North Terrace still meets both needs. The new buildings on North Terrace, at its western end, are sustainable, 'look at me' buildings for cutting-edge scientific and medical research and learning. It no longer has the Flower Day of the 1950s and 1960s, when school children donated flowers to be transformed into a great floral carpet display, a great community event in its day. I remember the early morning picking of pinky-gold Peace roses in my mother's scented garden; their petals were required for the floral carpet being made by the housewives of Adelaide. Now this stately street hosts much bolder festival events like the lightshows on its cultural buildings, which began in Adelaide at the 2002 festival. Screened then for the first time in Australia, they are now mainstream in festivals across Australia.

Behind tree-lined North Terrace lies Adelaide's first university, a red-brick campus unfolding down the hill with stairs and terraces. A little like an Italian hilltop town, it connects to the city's only river and the parklands beyond. Dame Roma Mitchell studied law at the University of Adelaide, where she no doubt determined that being a woman would never hold her back.

The University of Adelaide and North Terrace are important in my life. The university was the first grown-up place I was really free to wander and to explore new ideas and people, a place of freedom to learn and to be, a place where the constraints of an Adelaide girls school were removed. I made lifelong friends there. Later for me it became a place for giving back and participating in its governance by serving on the University of Adelaide Council. My appointment to the council was made by its first woman vice-chancellor, Mary O'Kane, who looked up to Dame Roma Mitchell as a role model, as all professional women in Adelaide did. I remember Dame Roma's advice to me when I was trying to balance the competing interests of a political life as a city Alderman, Deputy Lord Mayor, wife and mother of two small boys. It was simply: 'don't fret and things will always work out'. It was the kind of understated common sense advice she always gave, although this advice was not always easy to follow for a young, impatient, ambitious woman.

Mary O'Kane is still the only woman in almost two hundred years to have held the role of vice-chancellor at the University of Adelaide. Her legacy was a master plan that rethought the campus for the next fifty years and more by planning a series of new buildings to meet the teaching needs of the twenty-first century. She was not afraid of change and wanted Adelaide's university to be world class in every way and supported opening its connection to the life of the city and the wider community. With the plan drawn up by her friend Aldo Giurgola, the architect of Australia's Parliament House in Canberra, she left an expansive blueprint that has shaped the campus into a contemporary institution much more open to the city and its citizens but retaining its eminence and history.

Mary O'Kane liked to shock the conservative Adelaide community. Her portrait by Adelaide artist Anna Platten was twice the size of the portraits of her male predecessors. It caused a stir on North Terrace and in university circles. She was painted in a business suit with a characteristic short skirt, showing good legs, with an adder slithering past. Described as 'a progressive portrait of an empowered woman' in the curator's notes in a retrospective of the artist's work at the Art Gallery of South Australia, it captures the spirit of North Terrace as a place of empowerment and of art, learning, culture and intrigue, with room for progressive women.

It is the university where Australia's first woman Prime Minister has a place in the Faculty of History and Political Science, an appropriate haven for Julia Gillard to build the next stage of a career contributing to public life and community.

The close connection between the university and the public collections of the North Terrace museums, which house the treasures belonging to and given by the South Australian community gives North Terrace its particular energy: it is not any ordinary street. It is both a destination and a haven away from the streets of the city's mostly poorly designed, plain twentieth-century commercial tower blocks. It is the kind of main street that every town and city needs to lift the spirit of its community. By the early 1990s, when I was a member of the Adelaide City Council and crusader for heritage protection, North Terrace was an important heritage site being neglected. It was a street whose grandeur was taken for granted. Well into its second century it had been abandoned, and its revitalisation combines the old with the new in a story it is important to record. It is a story of women leaders and the community voice.

By the early years of the twenty-first century North Terrace had been reinvented, through the persistence of a group of strong, influential and determined Adelaide women being the drivers for change. I first heard the idea of renewing North Terrace at a Government House reception hosted by the governor, Dame Roma Mitchell, to launch a community group, 'Treasures on the Terrace'. At that time main streets were often the focus of heritage activists and planners for improvement, but this was a bigger idea. As a civic leader, I supported it. So many of the best ideas come from the community, who see potential in the areas and ideas which busy politicians often overlook. Politicians sometimes just need to listen. The Adelaide artist and former journalist, Winnie Pelz, who later went on to be head of the South Australian Department for the Arts for a time, was the first chair of the North Terrace Action Group, raising awareness amongst influential circles in Adelaide and gaining public support for the importance of North Terrace and its collections. This group had the quiet support of Dame Roma Mitchell. The North Terrace supporters called for improvements to the shared urban landscape, the gardens, paths and forecourts between the buildings as well as to the buildings themselves. But the streetscape was to come first. Much of the now-improved space was a kind of no man's land of shared neglect by the state government and the Adelaide City Council.

I played a small part in the story, along with other women who later influenced its transformation. One Monday night in council I spoke in support of a national design competition for a North Terrace master plan. This was a new idea in Adelaide in 1991. Designs were submitted, exhibited, worked over and rejected. I supported the winning scheme, which proposed the removal and replanting of tired gardens and ageing ash trees. I saw the new design as an improvement to North Terrace, one that would invite people into the cultural places dotted along its length. I learned a life lesson about how distrustful people can be of politicians proposing change; I also learned about the public's sensitivity to the suggested removal of trees from public places even to plant new ones. The design I supported became one of the key issues that caused me to later lose the Lord Mayoral election and my seat on the Adelaide City Council.

The momentum for change on North Terrace slowed for a while when I left the council. Like many good ideas and many public projects it languished. The next time it came back onto the agenda women were in charge. Jane Lomax Smith was Lord Mayor and Diana Laidlaw was the Minister for the Arts and responsible for almost all of the cultural institutions lining the Terrace. Her advisors, Winnie Pelz in the Department of Arts, and Janet Worth, worked together to coordinate improvements to the cultural museums and to North Terrace itself as a carefully integrated plan for the renewal of this important place in Adelaide. These four women were purposeful.

Taking the community along when making changes in cities is always a delicate balancing act. Having focused on preserving Adelaide's individual heritage buildings and the character of streets by calling for the introduction of local heritage listing, I had believed the community would be ready for improvements to the streets and squares in the inner city. But it was fifteen years too soon.

A less controversial planting scheme to beautify the city introduced by the council team at that time was the mass-planting of roses in the city's residential areas and the planting of plane trees on the city streets to give summer shade. Roses grow profusely in the heat of Adelaide and these are now, twenty years later, gloriously abundant in public gardens and along footpaths in the city and North Adelaide. They are part of the place-making legacy from a time when women were part of an independent council majority.

The North Terrace plans were revived when Jane Lomax Smith became Lord Mayor of Adelaide. She supported the arts festivals, the cultural life and the life of ideas, understanding that this is the essence of the Adelaide's spirit as a city – past and present. Jane Lomax Smith understood the importance of access to the culture and education that North Terrace could provide for people of all ages and walks of life. She describes North Terrace as 'the heartbeat of Adelaide' and recognises it as the centre of gravity in Adelaide. About North Terrace she says:

> It's a place that people can spend time in; it's where people are and where things happen. It has become a place where it's good to be. The cultural institutions have been drawn out into the shared spaces. They increasingly bring their activities outside and bring music and speeches and art onto the footpaths. It never came out before and now there are coffee carts, deck chairs and some days even pianos, and pop-up lunchtime cafés.

The new North Terrace shows how changing the spaces between the buildings in our towns, local neighbourhoods and cities can infuse new life into old places. The trick is to make them feel like places worth sitting in and walking along, to make them a living room. North Terrace remains and always has been a gathering place for the young, for students and for the intersection of ideas. It is like New York's Washington Square, a place filled with students while business functions around it. It has some of the student buzz of Sydney's Broadway and Glebe Point Road, where the University of Technology Sydney and the University of Sydney add a street life vibe of diverse and youthful energy. People occupy North Terrace in spite of, not because of, the very grand buildings. North Terrace makes inner-urban Adelaide seem a much bigger, younger and more diverse city than it really is.

Australia's cities have a few grand streets but they are not the centre point for community life in the way that North Terrace has become for the people of Adelaide. Melbourne has plane-tree lined Collins Street, with its trams, grand towers and the elegant international boutiques at its top end, sometimes called the Paris end of Collins Street. Collins Street has North Terrace's grandeur, but it is not a street embraced by the wider community as a cultural heart. It is a gracious place for business, fashion and style, but that's not for everyone. Federation Square has become the community hub of

Melbourne, but it's not a street. Sydney has Macquarie Street, with Australia's finest colonial architecture. I love the golden sandstone simplicity of St James's Church and the glorious green of Hyde Park at one end and the great wonder of the Opera House at the other, which ends the street like a glorious crescendo by the harbour. It is one of Australia's best streets. But it is not a meeting place or a place to gather. Neither of these wonderful streets is a daily meeting place in the way that North Terrace has become in the past few years, with its university, museums, galleries, libraries and gardens and their cafés. It has always been a retail street with major department stores and a few exclusive clothes shops but it is the cultural life of North Terrace that defines the place. It is the mix of spaces, museums, galleries and cafés that works like a magnet to attract people of all ages. While tasting the local wine is probably the top of the visitor 'to do' list, visiting North Terrace is next.

Across the world there is a focus on making public spaces in cities places that are attractive and welcoming. In London public places are being reshaped to meet the demands of the new 'millennials', the generation choosing inner-city urban life. Similar to the North Terrace Project, which made the empty spaces and lanes around the cultural buildings inviting, one of the most successful reclaimed spaces in London is a transformed empty inner square, a void between the exhibition spaces and storage at the back of the Victoria and Albert Museum (V&A). It is now a meeting place, with cafés, artworks, sunny summer lawns and a shallow splashing pond, a magnet to urban children. It is a space that makes you feel joyful and very much part of a community that claims the design world of the V&A as theirs.

During visits to London over the past few years, I have watched it become a public refuge in a busy city full of footsore travellers. It welcomes circles of students, lovers stretched on the lawn, mums, dads and grannies, toddlers and prams, or older people with coffee and a book, alone but feeling part of a connected humanity sharing London public life.

North Terrace exudes this same feeling. It is a success, now much awarded for its design. I have shared this story to ensure that the endeavours of the small group of persistent women determined to make this a better place are not forgotten, like so many of women's successes. The final design for North Terrace that was built came from the husband-and-wife partnership of landscape architects Taylor Cullity Lethlean. Kate Cullity and the late Kevin Taylor gave Adelaide a special gift.

North Terrace has the magic of new garden beds, with native plants as hedges and shading trees to give enclosure and softness amongst the grand architecture. The artists Angela and Hossein Valamanesh reset a fountain to create a new installation of beauty and delight. Without the drive of the women who imagined a better North Terrace, these designers might never have had the opportunity to undertake the project that invites us in through Adelaide's front door.

North Terrace still has the pageant that signals Christmas, holidays and a long hot Adelaide summer. Wandering North Terrace on an autumn afternoon I see the faded blue lines that contain the crowd at pageant time. Walking the terrace is now a cheering experience – bright French candy-striped canvas deck chairs dot the lawns in front of the South Australian Museum to resemble an English park. Students spend lazy afternoons on the grassy squares of the cultural institutions with a book or a friend, a rare thing in the main street of any city; at lunchtime people completely occupy the lawns, sitting in neat rows of timber seats as if in a park, not alongside a busy city street. Wild grasses and resilient plants thrive with little water, reminding me of the wilderness beyond the city; clipped hedges suggest the control and good manners of Adelaide society. Wild and mannered is a metaphor for North Terrace and perhaps for Adelaide. The new North Terrace gardens seem a perfect reflection of Adelaide's struggle as a city wanting the grace and civility of a European city while being at the edge of a desert and founded by dissidents wanting social change.

On North Terrace tourists can meander past one of Australia's rarest rows of street trees, the ancient dragon's blood trees, and walk close to the richly crafted limestone walls of Government House, pale-washed rough stones brought to order and capped with neat red brick to hold them tight. In front of Government House they may notice the plaques set into the pavement commemorating South Australian citizens of renown and achievement. They may stop to read and photograph the local heritage information and admire the statues. The poet Robert Burns is there, as is voluptuous Venus and the upright bust of the pioneering South Australian suffragette Mary Lee. They are an odd but interesting bunch and tell something of the values of South Australians.

The statue I love most is not a great work of art but captures the spirit of a great woman who loved North Terrace and all it represents. Dame Roma Mitchell sits in an Edwardian armchair surrounded by a stack of books, with a book on her knee, her hand holding her place while she looks up as if to give answers. Her biography, aptly titled *Roma the First*, written by Adelaide historian Susan Margery with Kerrie Round, tells the story of her outstanding achievements in public life. The book gives candid insights into this woman's thoughts as she transitioned from life as a Queen's Council to the role of first woman Supreme Court judge. Her thoughts show how human she was.

Later when she was appointed South Australian Governor she told the Adelaide *Advertiser*:

> It will take a while to get accustomed to the fact that I will have to live in more isolation and I won't be able to move quite as freely as I have in the past which I always like doing. I like moving among everybody.

On North Terrace, Dame Roma sits in a pair of Ferragamo flats, with her ankles neatly crossed. Female and yet strong, she is immortalised sitting upright, wisely, smiling in a garden. She remains an enduring model of grace and strength to all who wander past her. On the side of her statue, made by the sculptor Jeanette Moore and the Mylor Sculptors of the Adelaide Hills, are the words: 'Sapiens Qui Assidus Est'. (It is prudent to have patience.)

Patience is a life lesson, one of the hardest to learn. Making good places in cities takes both time and patience. Bringing about the change to remake North Terrace took patience and the change is still underway and will always continue. Cities are never complete.

North Terrace is an important street for women in Australia. The first parliament in Australia that first voted to allow women to vote and to stand for parliament sits on North Terrace. Perhaps it's not surprising then that a group of us who cared about this special place acted in its interests. In different ways each of the women associated with North Terrace had the passion, patience and persistence to serve public life and advocate for this fine historic boulevard to become the elegant, inviting and very public place it is today. We have succeeded in breathing new life and spirit into the place, ensuring that Adelaide's cultural heart continues to beat strongly.

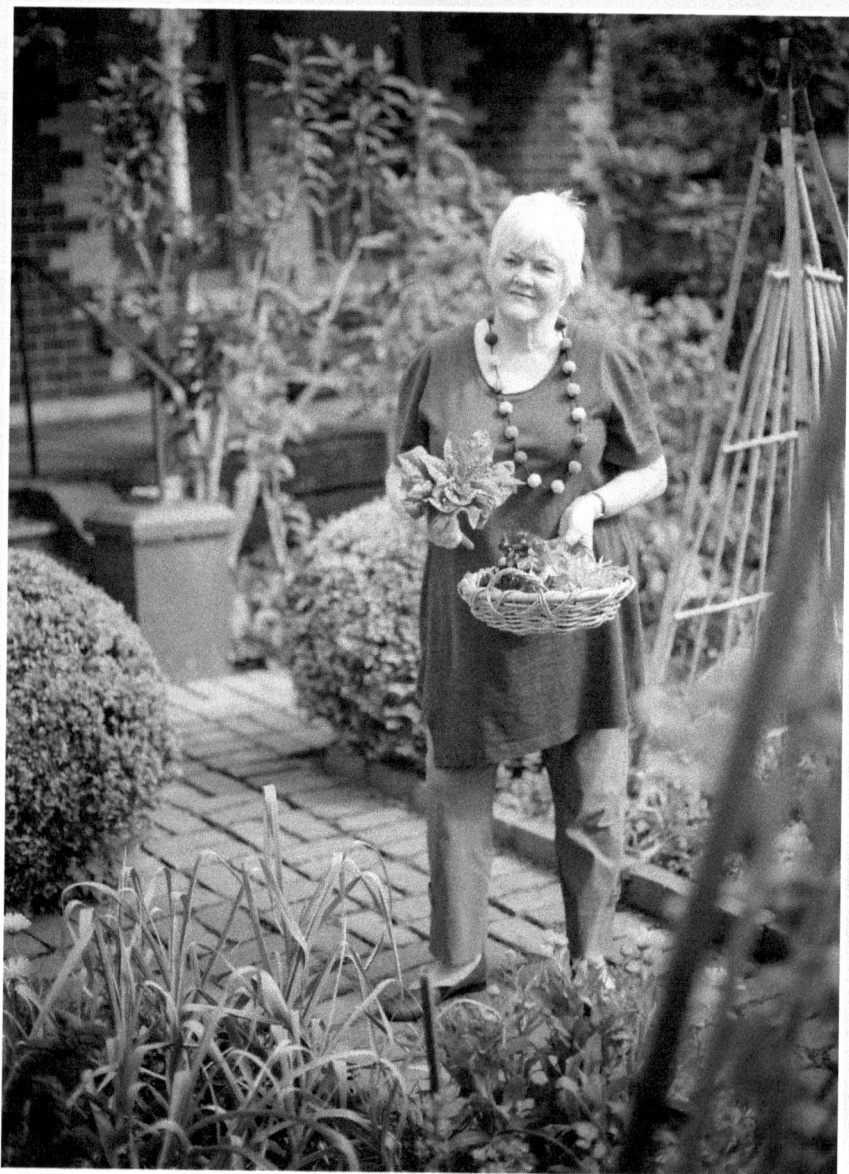

STEPHANIE ALEXANDER, *harvest in hand; a cook, a gardener, a community educator who popularised growing and eating good food.*

URBAN
HEROINES

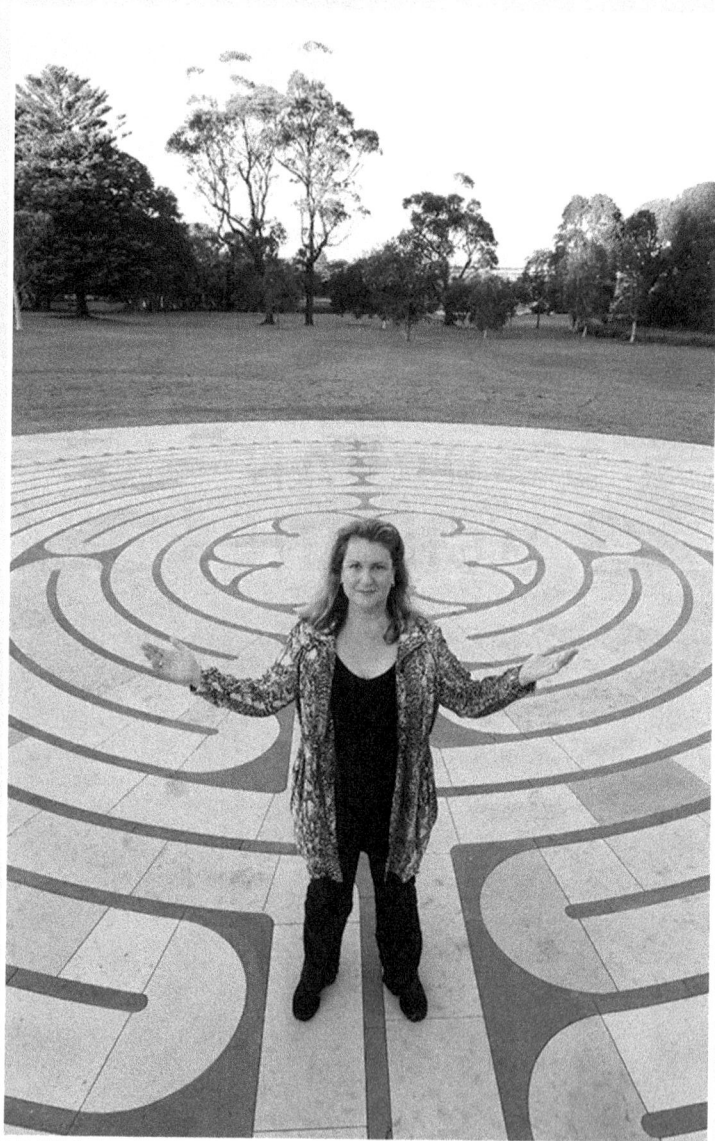

EMILY SIMPSON *walking the labyrinth she dreamed of making in Sydney's Centennial Park, a path for others to share.*

BEGINNING A MOVEMENT

It is solved by walking.

SAINT AUGUSTINE

There are women who have led movements that have changed
life in Australia. They share common qualities – imagination,
passion, a drive to help others to enjoy a better life and, crucially, a
belief that they can make change happen.

Grass-roots activists are vital in community life, and women
make great activists. They take an inter-generational view, with a
fearless, 'nothing to lose and much to gain' attitude, caring not for
themselves but for their community. Over and over again in the local
urban battles of Australia, stories abound of women fearlessly in the
front line defending their local ground; women are wonderful urban
activists. They are courageous custodians, who are persistent in their
support of a cause and encourage others to speak up about what
change is acceptable and what is not. Urban life is not only concerned
with places; it is also concerned with what cities allow us to do and
how they enable us to flourish. They let us work, connect, wander and
feed our curiosity and imagination.

With one school project in Melbourne's Collingwood College,
the Melbourne chef and gardener, Stephanie Alexander, began a
movement encouraging people to grow and eat healthy food. This led
to a burgeoning interest in food and the movement for community
gardens that has spread into suburbs across Australia. Sunday Reed

would surely have loved the work of Stephanie Alexander. In these community gardens, people can get together, make friends and learn to grow food. Community gardens do more than produce food, they are gathering places that bring purpose and fellowship to perhaps lonely people's lives; they are a way for kids in trouble to connect with others, do something of value and learn to eat better. Gardening is also a healing activity. More of Stephanie's story comes later.

Places grand and small are often created through activism. Sydney's great Opera House needed community activism to ensure its construction. Further around the harbour's edge to the west of the bridge in Pyrmont is a new urban park. The community of Pyrmont rallied against development and called for a park. Pirrama Park in Sydney's Pyrmont, with its inventive places for kids' play and students to party, is a shared backyard for people of all ages in one of the most densely populated apartment-dwelling communities in Sydney. Without the leadership of Clover Moore and the activism of a group of local women led by Marcelle Hoff, this wonderful gift would not have been realised. That is true of many small and local places that are loved in towns and cities across Australia. It takes one woman from a community to call others to action.

Marcelle Hoff led a local protest to stop the development of apartments on harbour-front land that she believed should be a community park. It was her aim to secure this park that led her to stand for the council. We met by chance, seated next to one another on a flight from Adelaide. She recognised me as the heritage activist I had been in Adelaide and asked my advice. I advised her that if she wanted the park the best way to get it was to stand for council, and she did.

Some activists look beyond their local neighbourhoods. A humanitarian activist with steely resolve, the architect Andrea Nield led a call to architects to create awareness of climate change and its impact on Australia's Pacific Island. The catalyst for her founding of Emergence Architects Australia was the 2004 Boxing Day tsunami that devastated Indonesia, and her aim was to help rebuild the shattered lives of the communities who had lost their homes from natural disasters – in Australia and beyond. Her belief is that this should be done in their communities, working at a village level and working with the materials and design that made sense in their lives, Nield believes that architects should do this sensitive work.

Nield called on Australian architects to design for the poorest communities devastated by the impacts of climate change. The organisation founded by her, Emergency Architects Australia, was closely linked to the successful French agency, Les Architects de l'urgence, and later helped to rebuild the community of Kinglake in Victoria after its devastation by fire in 2008. The organisation's architects also built schools and housing for communities in Samoa and Indonesia, places where tsunamis have destroyed community life.

Many of the women architects and urbanists I have worked with have taken up the cause of green activism and many have been fervent and effective communicators for their cause. The Sydney architect Caroline Pidcock is one. Her website carries messages to inspire, for example, the Kenyan proverb: 'Treat the earth well. It was not given to you by your parents. It was loaned to you by your children.' Caroline has built her practice and her reputation on being an advocate for sustainable design and living and is a green activist to her core, speaking at events and forums to build understanding about climate change and how we can act to live more lightly on the earth. Awarded the Marion Mahony Griffin Prize for her work in advancing sustainable design, Caroline has been an influence in Sydney, and nationally, on community debate about sustainability and what it really means in the design of our cities and how we live. She is a forthright advocate and continues to be an effective leader in the debate about climate change.

City development is a complex process and women who are good communicators can often cut through the noise of politics and planning with simplicity and clarity. The Aboriginal designer Alison Page speaks with great conviction when she explains why we can learn from the Aboriginal design process. As architect for a hospital for the Wilcannia community, she sat with the community and discussed their stories and their dreaming. She says the hospital was a place which Aboriginal people were not allowed to enter. In the building process the team trained six Aboriginal apprentices and it then became a place belonging to everyone. When discussing sustainable design, she says:

> Sustainability is inherent in our design. We treat the land like our family. Story and art is a must have in our design and culture. Story builds preciousness in objects and makes us keep things. The principles have a lot to teach others about sustainability.

It was heritage activism that drew me into shaping and influencing places in our cities, as it has many other women. In Adelaide the city council team I led was successful in advocating for the introduction of local heritage listing and a scheme for heritage conservation in the city. At the time the state government Planning Minister was a woman who took a long view, and that helped. Susan Lenehan, the Minister for Planning and Environment, and I met as women wanting to make a difference. We would walk and talk on the way to the gym under the Hyatt Hotel on North Terrace, where Susan exercised. We marched past the civic offices on Adelaide's Victoria Square down Adelaide's main street, multitasking as we planned to save Adelaide's colonial heritage. Susan, now living in Sydney, was willing to support the introduction of local heritage listing in the *City of Adelaide Planning Act*. It was a model to be tried in the inner city, before extending the legislation across metropolitan Adelaide. I am not sure how long it might have taken had it not been that the two of us were intent on solving a problem together. At the time the need to conserve the city's heritage character concerned the local community deeply, although property developers and owners were opposed to it. It took courage to take them on.

In 1993 a total of 1492 buildings, twenty per cent of the buildings in the heritage streets of Adelaide were listed for protection. Despite some objections from owners that were upheld, most are preserved and give inner-city Adelaide and North Adelaide a unique and much-admired character. These were streetscapes of cottages, row houses and villas which show how people had lived since the time of colonial settlement. Most dated from the mid-nineteenth century, with some dating from the early twentieth century. Saving the neat rows of colonial stone buildings was about maintaining the human scale of the place and bringing the past into the future. The cottages have more than held their value and many have attractive additions. Preserving Adelaide's heritage led to my defeat in the 1995 Lord Mayoral election.

Like many women who leave public life by choice or by losing elections, I became a commentator, remaining an activist for good design. I kept my voice by writing a weekly urban affairs column in Adelaide's local paper, the *Advertiser*. This is not the same as making decisions but it assists in shaping community views and influencing people. There is a long tradition of women writing about social issues in Australia, dating as far back to *The Dawn*, the magazine produced in Phillip Street in Sydney by Louisa Lawson, the mother of the great Australian poet Henry Lawson, and perhaps the forerunner of the *Australian Women's Weekly*. Today the new online journals such as those started by comedian and social commentator Wendy Harmer, *The Hoopla*, and *Anne Summers Reports* by the feminist Anne Summers are twenty-first century versions of *The Dawn*, in that they investigate what happens in Australian life through a woman's eyes.

The Dawn began in 1888 in the years leading to the dawn of Australia as a nation in 1901. It was named for the times, but her real focus was on issues that would lead to a new dawn for women and their rights in society. Similar to the women's magazines that followed it, *The Dawn* offered recipes and household advice, fashion, poetry and a short story and reported women's issues in Australia and abroad. It built an international readership amongst women in its promotion of women's suffrage, the right to divorce and equal rights at work. Financially successful, Louisa Lawson formed the Dawn Club, which was feminist to its heart.

As a young mother working from home I wrote for the *Women's Weekly*, today still one of the journals with one of the highest readerships in Australia – although it is now published monthly. Its editors influence its voice. Ita Buttrose famously advocated for women's issues, as has the editor Helen McCabe, a country girl at heart from the Clare Valley in South Australia, who for a time was a Canberra Press Gallery journalist. Once again the *Women's Weekly* covers social and political issues.

The Sydney architecture writer Elizabeth Farrelly would no doubt have enjoyed a meal with Louisa Lawson. Elizabeth's activism began as a councillor on the City of Sydney Council as a heritage supporter. Elizabeth is still tweeting 'Save Sydney's Sandstone'. When she left the council she turned to the pen to influence urban development in Sydney. A journalist, opinion writer and architect, she has been a real force in the development debate in Sydney, using her quick, sometimes shocking, wit and humour to raise issues, influence decision-makers and shape community thought. Elizabeth and I share being young and idealistic heritage activists and members of our respective city's capital city councils. Both of us were on pro-heritage teams, and were, like many who at that time stood for the local council, dismayed by the reckless removal of important heritage in Australian cities through the 1970s and 1980s. Back then, adapting heritage buildings was a way to ensure that places of beauty, interest and history survived. Now we recognise that adapting and reusing buildings is a smart and sustainable approach.

Elizabeth Farrelly's blend of commentary is a mix of design review and architectural critique, social observation, despair, politics and sheer entertainment and offers strong independent views on the civic players, the plans, the policies and the places. Melbourne has a counterpart in the architect and writer Dimity Reed, who has long played a role as an architecture critic in that city. Cities need informed voices and they need the perspective of women.

For more than twenty-five years, Stella De Vulder, a warm woman with a quick mind, has understood the important relationship between the community, architecture and design. A hero of community education on architecture and design in Australia, she became an advocate for the design cause, and architects in Australia have much to thank her for. As the woman behind the scenes, she masterminded the high-profile media coverage of Australia's leading annual awards for architecture, first written about by Peter Ward in the *Australian* decades ago. Understanding the psychology of architects and the value of architecture to our cities, she worked quietly and surreptitiously to facilitate public debate about the importance of good design and its benefit to a wider community. A growing number of women have now received professional awards for their contributions to improvements in our cities, although an equal number with influence go unnoticed and often unthanked.

Once the editor of the pro-development Property Council magazine, the journalist Tina Perrinotto jumped to the green side, attracting the developers to her online journal www.thefifthestate. com.au. Tina advances the cause of sustainability with an audience she knows, the property industry. She began an online journal years before social media started providing chat rooms about cities.

Maria Atkinson has been another kind of activist and advocate for sustainable change. The founding CEO of the Green Building Council of Australia, she set the agenda and established new standards for buildings by means of green-star ratings, collaboratively working with development industry leaders and government. She is a woman who has built her reputation on strident support for the case for change to more sustainable city-making. She made it her purpose to get involved with the top end of town and to influence political leaders. Maria Atkinson is an environmental scientist and an effective communicator for arguing for change and new thinking. She has lobbied for Australia's national agenda for sustainability and attended the Global Environmental Forums at Davos to influence policy. We met at the beginning of her public career as an advocate, when she was the first CEO of the Green Building Council of Australia, and have watched her rise in influence in the tough male-dominated world of property development.

The Green Building Council of Australia was originally the idea of another woman of influence in Sydney, one of Australia's few recognised women leaders in urban planning, Professor Sue Holliday. As the most senior planner in the New South Wales Government, Sue was in a position to seed-fund the Green Building Council at a time when Sydney was experiencing a population increase of 45,000 people a year and was challenged by the need for housing and office space. Her influence prompted the key developers in Sydney – and Australia – to adopt the 'green star' building principles. She cleverly encouraged a kind of competition between the developers to be first to build a five-green-star building, relying on the natural competitiveness of the boys to get them focused on more sustainable design.

Sue advanced the understanding of the construction industry about the global imperative to design sustainable buildings. New thinking in its the time, it is now mainstream, with the green-star building rating system a huge success. The mantra of Sue Holliday and Maria Atkinson is sustainability. Both showed courage in leading on this issue in perhaps the most male-dominated industry of all, property development. Although many industry representatives and politicians now promote sustainable building and design, these women promoted this concept in the very early days. The Green Building Council continues in the hands of another woman, Romilly Madew. She, along with Maria Atkinson, has been a founding supporter of 1 Million Women, mentioned earlier, successfully started by Natalie Isaacs.

This sisterhood of smart women questions development proposals and calls for sustainable approaches. One of the most outspoken opponents of the idea of building a hotel on land reclaimed from the harbour at Sydney's Barangaroo was the former Deputy Lord Mayor of Sydney, Marcelle Hoff.

On occasions women have a single idea about creating a place or making a change that will assist in easing busy urban lives, and they end up leading a new movement. It usually happens by accident and then by example. The Sydney town planner, Joan Masterman, worked with architects in the 1970s and was one of the few women working at this time as an urban planner on major projects. With the architect Ken Latona she created and gave urban dwellers and others access to special places outside cities to restore tired bodies and souls. Overcoming a minefield of planning obstacles, Joan Masterman paved the way for the Cradle Mountain Huts and Walk and the Freycinet Experience in remote Tasmania. Thirty years ago her decision to invest in the Cradle Mountain initiative, designed by her partner, the architect Ken Latona, began a movement in eco-tourism. Joan says she doesn't believe the Cradle Mountain Huts Walk would have happened without her involvement because of the complex planning issues involved in building accommodation and walking paths in a world heritage area.

Joan Masterman grew up on the land and a love of the bush has remained with her. With an appealing blend of shyness and purpose, Joan Masterman is still the driving force of the Freycinet Walks and Friendly Beaches lodge on the stunning east coast of Tasmania, north of Hobart. The plan had been to design an escape from urban life that would revive and renew frayed city dwellers in the breathtakingly beautiful wilderness landscape of Tasmania. She explained to me that it was the first time that people on the mainland had become aware of the existence of the wilderness. 'They had no idea about the magnificent mountain landscapes, the huge trees of the temperate rainforest of Tasmania.' The Cradle Mountain Hut project in northwest Tasmania would make the famous landscape accessible to visitors while protecting and preserving the grandeur and beauty of the bush and its wildlife and set a standard for environmental tourism in Australia. Now it is a model embraced by the environment movement as a way to protect significant places while realising some economic return.

A few years later the team created the Freycinet Walk and Lodge, which would become known as the Freycinet Experience. These pioneering projects showed how eco-tourism could enable the landscape to be enjoyed and protected while supporting local employment that did no harm to Australia's fragile flora and fauna. Joan says:

> I come from the country and the idea was to make it like a house
> party where people might arrive and not know the other guests
> and stay in a shack that was warm and comfortable with scones
> at the end of a day of walking.

Joan explains that the Cradle Mountain huts were designed to be like
small farm houses, to sit almost invisibly in the landscape.

The guides, she says, remain the most important ingredient,
informing visitors about the landscape and protecting both the
wilderness and its creatures and visitors. She was a committed
environmentalist before the word sustainability swept the planning
world and was way ahead of her time in considering how the walks
would be guided to ensure the safety of visitors and that of the land.
Freycinet is a place for everyone, but it attracts worn-out prime
ministers, politicians, writers and celebrities, who are renewed
by the silence and beauty of the landscape. As an aside, Joan
Masterman tells me that more women than men do the walk and, if
visiting the place to recover from sadness or exhaustion, they often
have an epiphany.

Joan was a town planner at a time when there were fewer
women in authority or involved in the business of making places in
cities. She reflects that it was not until she was part of a group called
Constructive Women that she found her voice. Exploring ideas with
like-minded women gave her professional confidence, which had
been silenced by being the thinker but not the presenter of work done
with men. 'At that time', she explained, 'women's voices were almost
never heard in local government meetings'. She maintains that
women are more skilled in listening and communicating. Sorting
out the battles amongst children at home makes them ideal planners
and strategists, capable of finding common ground in contested
development proposals. She claims:

> People in strategic planning are underestimated in the skills they
> require. There are layers of issues. I think women are often better
> in taking all the issues seriously. As women we have to manage so

many situations in families and these skills are helpful in dealing with the complexity of urban projects.

Joan Masterman's Freycinet Experience has been described as unlike any other, a place where, by touching the earth gently, you can connect with yourself and with nature. The gift Joan Masterman gave was a model for a new kind of tourism, one that enabled city people to discover the restorative power of the Australian bush. This model has since been followed in places of beauty and in many conservation areas across the country, from remote Broome, to Smith's Beach near Injidup in Western Australia, to Kangaroo Island and the Flinders Ranges in outback South Australia.

Getting out of the city is one way of finding peace, but places for calm and reflection are also needed close to where people live. In earlier times churches across our towns and cities provided places for contemplation and renewal. As fewer Australians practise structured religion, new kinds of places are needed to enable people to get in touch with their spirituality. One Sydney woman has given her city a most public labyrinth.

Emily Simpson first walked a labyrinth in a state of grief. She had lost a marriage, a friend and her mother. Advised by an older woman friend and mentor that walking a labyrinth could quiet the mind, calm the senses and bring clarity of thought, she set off to the Nave of the Grace Cathedral in San Fransisco, one of two hundred public labyrinths in the United States. After she had walked it, she returned the following day and walked it again, for hours, finding peace, and as she describes it 'reconnecting with her heart'. Walking a labyrinth is a form of meditation in the tradition of pilgrim walks. The complex repetition of steps, silence and frequent turns is thought to bring balance to the mind; when people reach the centre they feel a sense of completion and peace.

Many labyrinths, like the one in the Grace Cathedral, are replicas of the famous labyrinth in France's medieval Chartres Cathedral. For four thousand years labyrinths have been used as paths of insight and self-reflection. Emily led labyrinth walks for small groups across Sydney, using a huge temporary canvas version of the sacred geometric circle. People of all ages and phases of life accompanied her on these walks. In the United States labyrinths are used in hospitals and clinics to promote wellbeing.

On a sunny spring morning a few years ago my family and I walked the labyrinth that Emily had marked out herself with a tennis court line marker on the grass in Sydney's Centennial Park. This was before the first stage of her quest to have a striking Sydney Sandstone labyrinth erected in the park. I attended the 'walking-in' of the labyrinth and watched Emily walk alongside church leaders from every faith. The labyrinth was built following her extensive lobbying and fundraising efforts. This quiet sacred place, with its ancient spirit and sacred geometry, now lies in the heart of Sydney's eastern suburbs in a corner of the park, for all to walk.

Emily Simpson's aim is to strengthen awareness of labyrinth-walking so that it becomes an Australian movement. The daughter of the philanthropist Caroline Simpson and as one of the younger generation of the Fairfax newspaper dynasty, she has inherited the tradition of giving to her community. Her aim was to help others to deal with the unhappiness and confusion of grief and to share the healing power of walking. Silently walking the labyrinth in Centennial Park, surrounded by a great ring of trees and birdsong, is a calming and restorative experience. Emily is quick to explain that a labyrinth is not a maze.

A maze gives people an anxiety attack by blocking them, confusing them and offering dead ends. Walking a maze is an intellectual exercise, while walking a labyrinth is a spiritual one. Labyrinths bring people into balance and show the path continues to an end point, like life, despite twists and turns.

A very different approach to giving urban dwellers an escape from their fractured city lives was to convert a country town into an 'out of town' retreat for lovers of books and reading. Similar to the eco-tourism concept of the Cradle Mountain Huts and Walk and the Freycinet Experience, it was an idea that could help an entire small community to have a stronger local economy and purpose, while providing an interesting and unusual destination for urban dwellers.

Tess Brady, writer, academic and former Adelaide publisher, although she is reluctant to take the credit for it, was a key driver for the creation of Australia's first book town: Clunes Booktown. The book town idea has rescued the town from an uncertain future in the twenty-first century. Clunes is joining places like Hay-on-Wye in the UK, where books, reading and writers' events and festivals are the heartbeat of the place. The town of Clunes, about three hours drive from Melbourne, was at its peak during the 1880s gold rushes in the mid-nineteenth century, when it was a destination for people from Asia, America and Britain. Now, after declining throughout the twentieth century, it has reinvented itself in the twenty-first and is again developing a positive reputation and economy, this time for its bookshops set in the historic streetscape. Its annual festival is a giant book bazaar and literary festival rolled into one. There were a few pointers to the possibility of a creative economy taking off, with *Mad Max* and *Ned Kelly* filmed in the main street, which returned pride to the town as people recognised the quality of its historic architecture. But the larger towns of Ballarat and Daylesford were still the ones to attract a crowd. Tess Brady joined with a small community group of tree changers to direct their creative energy into renewing Clunes. Now, Clunes, once almost a ghost town, is establishing an international reputation as the place to find rare secondhand and new books, small press publications and collectable books and a festival that is growing in size. It all started as a rural renewal project by a group of volunteers who were not book traders, and who accomplished it without government support.

Clunes Booktown reinvented itself on the back of a book festival held each year in May. It's a model that other places could adopt and adapt. This small community has created an out-of-town book retreat that is already part of an international movement of book towns. In Oregon in the US, there's a small town, appropriately called Sisters, which hosts the Sisters Outdoor Quilt show. Attracting thousands of quilters from across the US and beyond, it takes place on the first Saturday in July.

Urban life needs to be balanced, and escaping the city to connect with a slower pace of life away from the crowds and with nature or with the handmade is ideal. However, if escape is not possible, the simplicity of country life can be brought to the city. The slow food movement and the trend of eating at cafés in communal tables or on sofas and coffee tables arranged as though at home have been part of city life in the past few years. In essence, these trends reflect the need for human connection, which makes us seek the mood of our living room and kitchen in our cities.

Interest in food and in eating more sustainably have translated to interest in where food is grown and how it reaches the table. The community garden movement is on the rise in Australian suburbs and towns, along with home and balcony gardening. Making gardens was once only done at home, but now making community gardens is often a shared pastime. Once people were focused on their private house and garden, now their love of 'house and garden' extends beyond the gate to into the shared spaces of their community.

The Melbourne chef, restaurateur and food lover, Stephanie Alexander, has been a leader in teaching Australian children and families about growing, cooking and sharing good food. Her interest in food she says is in her DNA, handed down from her mother, who, she explained to me, considered food to be an important expression of culture. Stephanie grew up in a household that grew fruit, vegetables and herbs, kept cows and chooks for milk and eggs, and says it was not until she was older that she realised that not all families saw:

> growing, preparing and sharing food as paramount and primal. I despaired of the food lives of many around me, feeling not only did they eat badly often because they did not know how to turn simple ingredients into delicious dishes but they were fodder for the purveyors of convenience foods.

Ten years ago Stephanie combined her imagination, hard work ethic, sense of fun and her influence to begin a program in schools when she saw official strategies failing to combat the obesity crisis for young Australians. 'Their messages were about caution, food pyramids and no one mentioned the pleasure of eating well.'

Now Stephanie Alexander's Kitchen Garden Foundation has support from state and federal government health authorities and can be found in schools across Australia, and includes some special programs in Indigenous communities. Stephanie explains that her program teaches young children 'to learn how important the table is, being together around the table is a learning for life'. The turning point she says was the publication of her book *The Cook's Companion*, which spread the message about eating well and sharing around the table. The book has certainly been my companion for many years. She claims that the book gave her authority not only amongst those who might have visited her Melbourne restaurant, Stephanie's, or the Larder café. Her aim, she says, 'was to raise awareness of how easy it can be to eat well and how important it is for our health and happiness'.

The community gardens that are popping up in neighbourhoods across Australia's suburbs are a movement inspired in no small part by Stephanie Alexander. She does not claim the movement as her sole initiative, but her skill as a communicator and the work of her Kitchen Garden Foundation have spread the message about eating well and understanding how and where food is grown. The foundation funds schools in the program to cultivate kitchen gardens – where children learn to work as a group to grow food, and how to cook it and then gather around the table to share and eat well. 'Kitchen gardens, community gardens and the wellbeing of being together and making something grow are part of learning to eat well and be healthy', says Stephanie.

From one side of Australia to the other, the farmers' markets of growers' produce now make weekend life richer for the urban dweller. In all neighbourhoods, from Sydney's crowded Kings Cross and Eveleigh Market, to the farmers' market at Melbourne's Collingwood

Children's Farm and South Australia's Willunga Farmers' Market, to Subiaco Farmers' Market in Perth, growers' markets attract huge crowds. They reflect Stephanie's influence. It is with great pride that she explains that the Harvest Picnic, which she masterminded as Melbourne's community celebration for Australia's Bicentenary in 1988, was the precursor of farmer's markets: 'It was the first and was a huge success'.

Having satisfied the palates of food lovers from Melbourne and beyond for twenty-one years of fine dining in her restaurant, in 1990 she opened one of Melbourne's first breakfast cafés. 'The Larder opened in 1997 and was a warm, friendly, neighbourhood place to eat and drop in to buy cheese in a cold room.' The kitchen garden project began a few years later, tapping into the curiosity, energy and eagerness of children to plant and watch food grow. She believes that community growing 'enriches people's lives'. Working together is also an important part of what is taught – as well as eating well.

> There is no doubt that doing things together in groups when people have a plot or a community garden gives people enormous pleasure and they make new friends. Whenever I venture forth to join a community activity, a gym, a choir or a French class I do benefit and feel a lifting of the spirit separate to the benefits of the specific activity.

Taking a different approach to ensuring people are able to eat well, the Adelaide activist and urban planner Stephanie Johnston has taken on the challenge of ensuring that Adelaide will always be surrounded by the agricultural land that is its food bowl. Using the available legislation and heritage listing, she is spearheading a movement to achieve protection for places the community values; the aim is for the landscape around Adelaide to be the Southern Hemisphere's first bid to be a UNESCO World Heritage listed landscape, joining places like Italy's Tuscany.

Stephanie Johnston is driven to protect this valuable asset for future generations and has advocated for the introduction of character preservation legislation for Adelaide vineyards and the beautiful hills region, an idea from local farmers and grape growers. Recognition for the regions surrounding the city of Adelaide is a step towards giving world recognition to the beauty of this gentle Australian landscape and its quality as an agricultural food bowl. Talking about the campaign, she gives credit to three women she describes as 'the dames of the Barossa' – Margaret Lehmann, the wife of the late wine maker Peter Lehmann, Janet Angas, wife of a descendant of George Fife Angas, after whom the Barossa town of Angaston is named, and the celebrity chef Maggie Beer. Johnston says all instantly understood the importance of getting behind the idea.

The work of women in cities so often begins with a simple idea and drive. What happens is often something far bigger than the original idea as first conceived. The women's shelter movement arose in the wave of feminism that arrived in the earlier 1970s in Australia, part of a new sisterhood formed worldwide to seek equality for women. In Sydney, the late Robyn Kemmis and feminist icon and journalist Ann Summers were among a group of women who squatted in two cottages in Sydney's Glebe. One of the cottages was called Elsie and so it became Elsie Women's Refuge and began a movement. It was closed by government decades later. Lord Mayor Clover Moore and Deputy Lord Mayor Robyn Kemmis were behind the naming of a nearby laneway Elsie Walk as a poignant tribute to the name of a place that is said to have been Australia's first women's refuge.

All the women I've met who have influenced change and led movements have immense energy, a sense of purpose and determination. They have seen no alternative but to succeed. It is said that if you believe that you can, you are halfway there. I'm certain many of the best places in our cities have become a reality because women are led by a passion for what they dream is possible.

Women are at the foundation of so many community events. Adelaide Writers' Week, which became the model that all the others followed, was in the hands of one woman, Rose Wight, for decades.

Women are natural volunteers, workers with passion, and many now lead in local government roles across regional and metropolitan councils, which only twenty years ago were filled mostly by men. Women have traditionally played the role of organising the fair or the school bazaar, the trading table or the community day fundraiser. Men help, but in my experience, women drive these community events and have for centuries. Wendy McCarthy, a leader, community activist and feminist, agrees with me. She shares a simple story from the time when she returned from living in London to the north shore of Sydney in the 1960s.

> The women of the neighbourhood found public land and decided to create one of the early adventure playgrounds. We enlisted the husbands to do what we couldn't do and mine built the flying fox. Without the activism of women it would never have happened.

I hear stories like these repeated over and over again as I talk to women: men were part of it but the movement for change wouldn't have happened without the women.

HEROINES FOR HERITAGE

Don't it always seem to go that you don't know what you've lost till it's gone ... they paved paradise, put up a parking lot.

JONI MITCHELL, 1970

People care about the street in which they live. In the 1970s the battle to save Australia's heritage and the environment movement swept through Australia's inner cities as development threatened streets and neighbourhoods. It followed, as with many social trends, what was happening in America. Everyone, no matter where they lived, began to care about the development that threatened nature and the heritage places in cities and in the country.

People found their voices as activists. They had been brought up on the protest songs of the Woodstock concert, Bob Dylan, Joni Mitchell, Joan Baez and others. In America in the 1960s the First Lady took up the cause of heritage, giving it respectability – and women followed; she was a woman who had set style and led fashion, and with her husband as President, she led social change.

Jacqueline Lee Bouvier Kennedy Onassis is one of the women in history I would most like to have dined with. Best known for her style, her pearls and pillbox hats – and her husbands – she is less often recognised as a pro-heritage activist and publisher. She cared about history and heritage, believing that respect for the past offers hope for the future. She used her position of privilege and education to take up this cause. When she lived as a young First Lady in the White House she was determined to save heritage buildings from demolition.

JACKIE KENNEDY ONASSIS *made heritage fashionable. As Mrs Kennedy,
she restored the Diplomatic Reception Room at the White House in 1961;
later she would save New York's Grand Central Station from the wrecker's ball.*

She saw the importance of preserving the neglected White House and restored its grand public and private rooms, bringing original furniture out from storage, returning the original furniture to the places it once stood. She also sought out missing pieces. In the White House the First Lady established an atelier where the furniture was restored and re-upholstered.

All the women, well known or not, who have campaigned against inappropriate development and to save heritage buildings have showed great courage, often being threatened for their beliefs. Jackie Kennedy took on the heritage battles when only in her early thirties. As First Lady she made it her first task to return the White House to a place of historic significance. She worked in different ways to preserve, protect and contribute to America's cultural heritage, campaigning to save private property in Washington's historic Lafayette Street, which was to have been demolished to make way for redevelopment. The great American urbanist Jane Jacobs had protested to save Penn Station, and, as the leader of a group of prominent New York citizens, Jackie Kennedy as a citizen of Manhattan, led the opposition to the destruction of the grand New York Central Railway Station, which was to be replaced by planned development. Imagine New York without Grand Central Station! She couldn't. Yet it must have taken great courage to speak up against such major development and the many millions of profit to be made in the heart of New York. At the launch of the protest she said: 'If we don't know about our past we cannot hope for our future'. In common with many less famous women, she was willing to speak out for the city she loved and chose to live in. Given her wealth and private nature, the purposeful public advocacy for protecting private property that was important historical architecture invited conflict into her life that she might have easily avoided.

Jackie Kennedy adopted New York as her home as a thirty-four-year-old widow and chose to bring up her children there; she also chose to become involved in community life. She supported a whole range of heritage-related activities that led to renewal of the unique

JUANITA NIELSEN, *journalist, heiress, activist, Sydney's heroine for heritage buildings, who lost her life for the cause. 'In case we ever need a picture of me, this is the one I want used,' she told David Farrell, 16 July 1975.*

Broadway Theatre district and the preservation of its theatres, also supporting the work of the Central Park Conservancy, whose aim was to make the park a safe and beautiful place for all community members. The New York Public Library was another of her causes. The places she campaigned to protect and preserve are now places that richly serve the urban inhabitants of Manhattan. She was a role model to women in New York, demonstrating the importance of women becoming involved in civic causes; she made it chic to be an activist. American actresses in our celebrity culture use their fame and glamour to influence by taking up political causes. The Australian actor and feminist, Cate Blanchett, is effective in her chosen role of influence and civic leadership in Australia: she was an early supporter of action against climate change. These women see that the past is linked to the future and understand that we only get one chance of preserving our heritage and the environment.

Juanita Nielsen, Australia's murdered heritage activist, was an heiress like Jackie Kennedy. She was the daughter of the English-born heir to the Mark Foys retail wealth. Beautiful, rich and well-educated, Juanita travelled, married, divorced and returned to live in a Sydney terrace at 202 Victoria Street, Potts Point. Seen as stylish yet bohemian, she began an alternative newspaper, NOW, in Sydney's Kings Cross and Potts Point. She cared about her street and her city.

Juanita Nielsen used the paper to campaign to halt a development that would erase the character of the ordered terraces houses and tree-lined streets perched along a ridge in Victoria Street, Potts Point. She disappeared on 4 July 1975 and is believed to have been kidnapped and murdered, although her disappearance has never been solved, with many documentaries and books compiled about what is still regarded as an unsolved murder. A childcare and community centre at nearby Woolloomooloo named in her memory has been rejuvenated for inner-city families by Sue Barnsley and Rachel Neeson under Clover Moore's watch.

Her activism and shocking unsolved murder was a wake-up call. She triggered a movement in Australia for heritage conservation.

I am reminded of her whenever I look across from one of the city's boardrooms to the ridge above Woolloomooloo and the cliff of very ordinary apartments that replaced the early grace of the grand Victorian terraces of her street. When I hear her name blasting from the tourist buses passing my Potts Point apartment, with their loud speakers praising the heritage buildings that remain I think of her innocent hope that people making cities would listen and take a long view.

So many Australian cities have lost vast swathes of their heritage architecture. Perth has bulldozed much of the nineteenth-century architecture of the inner city. Some say Sydney, Brisbane and Perth are more like American cities, while Hobart, Adelaide and Melbourne retain a British sensibility from colonial times. I don't really agree. Sydney is still rich in the history of first settlement. The streets and patterns of settlement and housing up to the mid-twentieth century mostly remain. The terraces of the inner-city suburbs, the federation semi-detached houses and villas, and the later Californian Bungalows ripple out from just beyond the harbour. There is important national heritage at Parramatta, where Sydney was first settled, which needs care and attention. Sydney has been too distracted by the new to fuss too much about the past and too pleased with views of the beautiful harbour to keep many of the gracious early mansions and their terraced gardens which once circled the harbour's edge, but the city still has Georgian jewels from its colonial times, like St James's Church and the Barracks on Macquarie Street.

In 1988, at Australia's Bicentenary, there was a moment when Australia's heritage came of age and was seen as important, and nowhere more so than in Sydney, where the Historic Houses Trust joined the National Trust of Australia (New South Wales) in preserving and caring for Australia's national heritage from the first days of settlement. Wendy McCarthy, an activist for many causes, worked on the Bicentenary and then went on to run the National Trust, strengthening its voice as a public custodian for heritage, to be followed by Elsa Atkin. Elsa Atkin tuned in with the zeitgeist and reignited the National Trust as an effective advocate for heritage conservation and consolidated the already strong movement.

The National Trust of Australia (New South Wales) had been started in Sydney by Annie Wyatt, an activist who was born in Redfern in inner Sydney in 1885. She campaigned to save bush on the north shore of Sydney from being razed for development and she took up the cause of a number of neglected Georgian mansions in Sydney. The prospect of the demolition of Burdekin House, a fine Georgian House on Macquarie Street, so incensed her that she proposed the idea of a trust, whereby buildings and landscapes could be permanently owned and protected for the enjoyment of the community. In 1945 the National Trust of Australia (New South Wales), modelled on the British equivalent, was formed. Other states followed and a national movement for the preservation of heritage places, inspired by Annie Wyatt, continues today. Women like Annie Wyatt, passionate about preserving historic buildings and rare gardens and landscapes, have been the energy of the National Trust ever since.

Through the 1970s and 1980s community activism was saving tracts of Australian bush and heritage buildings. Many of the people leading these battles to save familiar landmarks, buildings and precious bush were women and we can thank them for speaking up to preserve many of the places Australians now treasure as part of our built and natural heritage. The rows of Georgian-scale houses in the Rocks would have gone. Elsa Atkins at the National Trust campaigned to save the wharves at Hickson Road, which are now part of Sydney's cultural ribbon. She says it was women, educated and uneducated, who cared and protested and organised the green bans that saved the Rocks. Now the early terraces that show how people first lived in European settlement in Australia remain and have been reinvented as housing or as cafés, restaurants and B&Bs in the tourist hub the Rocks has become.

In 1988, the year of Australia's Bicentenary, the first and only woman Lord Mayor of Brisbane, Sallyanne Atkinson, was elected. She led the Expo Development, which began to change Brisbane from the big country town it was then. Sadly, in Brisbane, as in Perth, the push to develop in the 1980s meant the loss of irreplaceable heritage. The women elected at that time joined the men who ran the city and tried to equal them in promoting development, at almost any cost. In the spirit of equal opportunity for woman that was current at the time, Adelaide too had its first woman Lord Mayor, developer Wendy Chapman. She cared little for heritage or environmentalism.

It was in Melbourne where the first woman Lord Mayor, the architect Leckie Ord, established policies to protect the heritage of the city. Senior planners in Melbourne who were insiders at the time claim that her influence was pivotal in introducing the policies to protect heritage buildings and for promoting good urban design. Today Melbourne is a leading city in the world's liveability stakes. During her time on the council she initiated more than heritage conservation, she began strategies for city living, public art and a new approach to the river, all of which were designed to make the city a more liveable and enjoyable place. It could be that she began a movement, that of valuing and restoring heritage streetscapes. It was another campaigner for heritage, the lively, well-connected Lord Mayor, Winsome McCaughey, who advanced with great success what Leckie Ord had begun.

Michelle Grattan in the *Age* described Winsome McCaughey as 'a single mother' and 'feminist' who 'filled the town hall with shrewd women who acted as her support network'. It is clear when talking to Winsome that she was passionate about her city and community, the value of the precious heritage architecture of Melbourne and the tradition of Melbourne as a grand Australian city. It's also clear she was wholly committed to developing the city as a place for people. A leading Victorian urban planner told me that these women got the right people into the Town Hall. They supported the appointment of urban designer Rob Adams, who in his book *Grids and Greenery: The Character of Inner Melbourne* for the Melbourne City Council presented a manifesto for a new take on Melbourne. This stylish city of laneways and urban life owes much to Rob Adams and the thinking begun at this time. The celebration of Melbourne's heritage streetscapes and the preservation of small street blocks and laneways set a course that has largely continued since that time, leading to the successful urban design model followed by many Australian cities and towns. We can thank these women for the heritage movement that saved the laneways, which would later be enlivened by bars, galleries and street art, representing the human-scale culture of Melbourne's city.

The Victorian goldfields in the 1880s created the wealth that built the city that called itself 'Marvellous Melbourne' – because of the number of its grand Victorian buildings. While the city laneways had simpler buildings, both the grand buildings and the colonial townscapes had, like Adelaide's North Terrace, become shabby. As Lord Mayor, Winsome McCaughey led a program of heritage restoration and urban design improvements in the city, with other cities soon following. With this new approach came a witty and sometimes quirky public art program, which also became popular across Australia. Building on the beauty and charm of the laneways and their simple buildings and warehouses in ways that preserved their grit and authenticity but without pretension has changed the character of the city, and changed how people use the city and enjoy the places between the buildings.

In Sydney the conservation of the heritage places of North Sydney has been important to two women mayors, who followed in the footsteps of independent Mayor Ted Mack. The first woman to be elected Mayor of North Sydney, Carole Baker, was followed by the long-serving Genia McCaffery.

Genia McCaffery will be remembered for supporting the restoration of Luna Park after a fire almost totally destroyed this extraordinary Sydney landmark. Opposing schemes for redevelopment on the valuable waterfront site, she took on the role as the custodian of Luna Park, arguing that it should be maintained as a pleasure ground for generations of Sydney children, as well as a remaining a remarkable city landmark at night, as it flashes its mad smile across the bay to drinkers and flaneurs on the Opera House concourse.

It was not just heritage buildings that communities fought for. The headland parks in Sydney give the harbour beauty. In the 1970s a group of educated housewives from the Sydney suburb of Hunter's Hill met and formed an activist group that became known as the Battlers for Kelly's Bush. Betty James, a housewife and journalist who had moved from Adelaide, became a leader amongst her neighbours in the protest to protect the bush. Kelly's Bush was scrub in their suburb that grew to the water's edge. A plan by developer AV Jennings proposed housing on the twenty-four-acre site. The women decided to stop it through protest, and they did. The trade union movement, led by Jack Mundey, supported them with the first green bans forbidding work on the site. It was at this time that the environmental movement in Australia began to emerge, with its battles to save the bush and to create national parks. It was also the time that sand mining on Fraser Island, on the edge of the Great Barrier Reef, was halted, as was the building of the Franklin River Dam in southwest Tasmania, preserving the priceless wilderness for future generations.

The Battlers for Kelly's Bush recognised that the AV Jennings proposal was wrong. They spoke up with courage and acted to prevent it. Winsome McCaughey, explaining to me how she became elected to the Melbourne City Council, said it was when the government removed the local council: 'It felt wrong to lose the people's voice and we formed an action group at my kitchen table on a Sunday afternoon to watch development proposals'. She led formal objections to the removal of heritage buildings on Collins Street. Appearing before the commissioners and frustrated by not being understood about why the removal of a single heritage building mattered, she went to the bathroom and blacked out her front teeth and came back with a smile, to explain buildings like teeth needed to remain intact – as a row.

In Adelaide, when I was Deputy Lord Mayor, the community formed a picket line to prevent the demolition of a grand bluestone building known as the House of Chow. I learned years later that the night vigil had been the idea of the wife of one of the leading surgeons at the Royal Adelaide Hospital; she was educated, stylish, articulate and outraged at the loss of Adelaide's colonial buildings. She lined up with unionists and students, keeping vigil all night and feeding the picket line with homemade soup, because she cared.

Being able to listen to communities and to hear and pass on their needs and opinions has been a key part of my work for twenty years and has shaped community-endorsed policies for planning and development. Women working in the haphazard world of shaping places are led by love for their community and for the desire for good places in cities. In modern city-making female approaches can bring a fresh and welcome change to this process. We need to listen and talk with local communities. We need to create places that help to preserve our urban memory and let us connect. Cities will continue to change and we must continue to learn from other places and find ways to preserve heritage places by reinventing them.

Cities and communities are full of problems to be solved. Design can provide solutions, but community voices need to be heard first. Women understand that human life is part of a continuum and that if we act today we can make a difference for tomorrow. Cities are not static; they are moving and changing all the time. Apart from the planners, urban designers and architects I have worked alongside, the women I have seen participate in the politics of the city became involved because they cared about the place in which they lived with their family and friends. Very few at the time had plans to become activists or to take on the challenge of being a local politician. The many women who have saved heritage buildings and protected great places have generally not been in public office, yet they have helped to preserve heritage and made our cities better places in which to live. Some have been writers, journalists, teachers and housewives and most are great communicators. The Sydney writer Delia Falconer championed a local community movement to prevent changes to the gardens surrounding the famous Kings Cross daisy fountain. The new plans were halted by the community. The Kings Cross daisy fountain, which never fails to lift my heart, was restored and will be maintained as central to any future changes to the gardens.

Sometimes the changes proposed go too far and a good communicator will quickly rally a community to action. Now social media spreads the word quickly. The need for the home-produced flyers and posters of 1970s activism is no more. Social media enables people to assemble quickly around common values; all that is needed is one effective communicator to lead a movement and invite a whole community to be heard. In the 1970s the Australian poet Judith Wright was also an activist in Brisbane and used her skill with words and her literary prominence to voice the need to save heritage buildings in the old Brisbane suburb of New Farm, a place that rises above the red cliffs of the wandering Brisbane River and still offers a memory of what Brisbane must once have been like. Although from a conservative grazing family, Judith Wright was an activist for the land rights of Aboriginal Australians and a land conservationist.

The Sydney writer Ruth Park lived through the demolitions of early colonial and Victorian workers' terrace houses in Surry Hills, writing about it and of the displacement of families as a way to try to stop it. These were the apartments whose construction Juanita Nielsen failed to stop, ugly and monstrous buildings blotting the views to the east for the city's most valuable offices and keeping the street in a permanent shadow of gloom, as if in mourning grey for Juanita Nielsen.

My fight for heritage began more than twenty years ago. At a dinner party I berated a friend who was a member of the Adelaide City Council. I was frustrated by the prospective loss of Adelaide's heritage architecture, the poor design of new development, the constant threats to build on Adelaide's parklands and the lack of consultation with people about all these issues. He challenged me to run for council. I did. It changed my life. Among the buildings saved was the Queen's Theatre, the oldest mainland theatre in Australia, which had faced demolition.

As a young city Alderman I took on the tough role as an activist and led a ferocious public debate about the need to protect and list as local heritage buildings that might not be grand and ornate items of state heritage but demonstrated how the small streets, row cottages and laneways and the grander villas of colonial settlement and life in Adelaide had begun.

The argument for demolishing heritage was the same in Adelaide as it is the world over. These were ordinary cottages that had been lived in by workers, and were considered not worth keeping, not grand enough to be important. But these streets of early row cottages and houses have gained in value, and the fight to keep them seems more significant now, with their obvious contribution to Adelaide's charm and mood as a city.

When I first became passionate about leading change in cities I was a young mother and a feminist and as a feminist I had remained Jane Jose even after marriage. But when I decided to stand for my local council to save the heritage architecture of Adelaide I was advised to do it as Mrs Rann. In the six years I served on the Adelaide City Council I was Councillor Rann, Alderman J.M. Rann and then Deputy Lord Mayor Rann. The titles were not designed with women in mind. When I was swept into council with a large vote in 1989, I joined a governing body that had seen only a handful of women elected in 175 years, and it was less challenging for the men who held power that I was a 'Mrs'. The team I worked with was mainly women. They were a group of smart, effective, courageous and principled women.

The polyglot forensic pathologist and wonderful orator and storyteller, my friend Jane Lomax Smith, has me to blame for recruiting her to public life. She would outstay me, to become Lord Mayor and a state government minister. I encouraged her to join the pro-heritage team when she was an elegant multi-tasking breast-feeding mother and practising pathologist. The late Rosemary Boucaut, with wisdom and kindness, supported me on to the council, provided balance and always saw the funny side of life. She was the driving force behind the rose planting that gives North Adelaide some of its charm.

Jackie Shannon Gillen, also part of the team, was then a young, passionate environmentalist and architect who had worked as a strategist for the rock singer, conservationist and later Australian

Government minister, Peter Garrett, when he was the hip president of the Australian Conservation Foundation and lead singer in Midnight Oil. Another in the team was Francene Connor. Bright and ambitious, she was a resident who wanted to contribute to her city. She came on to council, replacing a planning lawyer who had been tipped as future Lord Mayor and who is a lifelong friend, Mary Lou Jarvis. Unlike me, Mary Lou is still active in mainstream politics, having been a strategic advisor to the inspired public leadership of her local member of parliament, Malcolm Turnbull.

We were the unlikely group of women who joined in an alliance committed to preserving Adelaide's heritage and making community life richer. Our photographs still line the walls outside the council chamber, along with those of a number of other women, including Anne Moran and Professor Judith Brine, whom I encouraged to stand for Council.

We would not have succeeded in the heritage battle to win a majority of seats in the Town Hall without the support of a local community heritage activist group, the Aurora Heritage Action Group. Community activism now takes place online and in the streets and is vital if there is to be any real change in our cities. The Aurora Heritage Action Group was largely made up of educated middle class women and their husbands, who had been coerced into helping. It was named after the local landmark, the Aurora Hotel, a stone pub at one time on Adelaide's Hindmarsh Square, but replaced by a carpark. The group had a determined leader, an American academic and historian, Sharon Mosler. She had come from the Jane Jacobs school of environmental activism and protest. As an American in Adelaide, she was bewildered that the city could seriously want to demolish the heritage buildings that seemed to be one of its best assets, its colonial architecture. The campaigns, like those of many women activists I have since known, were plotted at the kitchen table. But we were most certainly not housewife 'nobodies', as Jane Jacobs was accused of being.

I had purpose and passion, and the energy and anger born of grief from the loss of stillborn children and of my mother at the young age of fifty-six. I see now that her death made me realise that time can run out and this prompted me to act, to be a player and to contribute. I've never lost the feeling that our time is finite and we need to spend it well. I learned younger than many women to trust my inner voice and my heart, to say it as I saw it and to live everyday as a gift. I was without political experience, but at that time I led enduring change in one Australian city.

Standing for local council is not for everyone. Influence can be as powerful as being in the political arena and it is much more comfortable. Yet now, more than ever, good people need to run for public office, but for women it is sadly still an especially tough gig.

In the Australian cities and towns where heritage houses remain, young families want to live in them. In Sydney, Brisbane, Canberra, Melbourne, Hobart and Perth what remains of early inner-city housing is prized. These places don't need to stay snap-frozen in time. Part of the fight has always been to get progressive planning laws that allow alterations and adaptive use.

In the early 1990s the inner-city buildings in Adelaide that had been assigned local heritage listing now tell their own story with their small blue enamel plaques, which can be read as people walk about the city and North Adelaide. I chose the cornflower blue of the plaques as one of my last tasks before the Lord Mayoral election I lost, also losing my seat on the Adelaide City Council, just before my fortieth birthday.

Protecting local heritage was just one aspect of a hope I had to make the city where my family had lived almost since settlement a more open, cosmopolitan and enjoyable place to live. Twenty years on, there are other legacies from that time, when a small independent majority and with the largest number of women ever on council since its founding in 1840 made decisions and set a direction for the city. They were not all huge changes but they have made a difference and made city life more attractive and comfortable. Shady plane trees lining the city streets and giving shelter from the intense summer heat;

the mass-planting of roses; the renewed elegance of North Terrace's cultural institutions; and a more urban inner-city life developed around the preserved heritage of Rundle Street East are the legacy. The preservation of Adelaide's heritage character – the grand and the humble – makes the city a richer and more interesting place to be.

Enraged by the steady removal of historic buildings from Adelaide's inner-city streets and the poor design of their replacements, I stood for the local council, not really knowing what I was in for. I had the idealism and optimism of youth. It was before I had read of Jane Jacobs and the environmental movements that had begun in the US. I won a seat on the council as an independent, to the surprise of my friends and family, and especially to the unwelcoming incumbent Lord Mayor, who described me as a housewife from North Adelaide! I think he was trying to say what was famously said to Jane Jacobs by a New York City Council administrator when she opposed a development; she was called 'a nobody', just a mother. The Lord Mayor was a self-made traditional Greek man and to him I was a housewife wanting to get involved in running the city, which was men's business! To their surprise I had beaten a well-known Adelaide late-night talk-back radio announcer, Bob Francis. The Lord Mayor and his supporters saw me as someone who would block development, or perhaps they just didn't like the idea of sharing power with a woman. It seems ironic that I have spent the decades since then working with communities and listening to their ideas and then moulding them into the shape of new development that meets these needs.

Developers like to paint a picture that people are either opposed to development or for wholesale development. Black and white. The process of development is fraught with so many competing possibilities that the best places will only be made by listening to the community voice. My wish is that I had been on the Adelaide City Council to help Adelaide rethink the plans for the Adelaide Oval. The oval could so easily have been kept as the unique world-famous heritage cricket oval in its garden setting – with the new mega stadium built in the southwest corner of the parklands and linked to the light rail system.

Now the gardens are gone and Adelaide has a stadium out of scale with the city.

Like many of the women I have observed opposing development, my commitment has simply been to sensitive design, design that considered the site, the local culture and the people. Development that preserves the best from the past makes places of humanity that improve and enrich life for everyone.

As cities grow we need them to be sustainable, because more housing is needed and land is precious. Not all of us will have the pleasure of our own gardens or the luxury of living in the low-scale communities Jane Jacobs advocated. Having access to the humanist qualities of the streets that are a pleasure to walk was what she hoped for. Street gardens and markets, flower stalls, public seats and street art will be important and even more so if we live high above in apartments. We recognise now that a loss of human connection results from cities designed in ways that isolate people and prevent their being part of 'village life'. We also know the fundamental need for shelter and for human connection to keep us healthy. While planners at earlier times celebrated the leafy suburbs, now we need the leafy urban village, and more than ever to feel part of a community. The city is now our living room. Cities must be for everybody. Everybody matters. This was the mantra of Jane Jacobs and in the work of making cities for people it is still the first and most fundamental principle.

During Jane Jacobs's adult life North American cities underwent transformation. As a young woman she would have seen the first great New York towers of the 1920s and 1930s begin to shape Manhattan into civilisation's first high-rise metropolis. She saw cities and lives changed as cars and freeways swallowed community neighbourhoods to enable growth. And she foresaw their impact on community life. It is important that her female way of thinking about cities stays with us. It is natural for women to think across the generations as part of our instinct to nurture and ensure the survival of our children and grandchildren. Women are always concerned with the survival of the species. We create life.

Now in cities we see the many new problems of a more transient and socially isolated society. We see people who are living longer and who are more often alone. We have the random acts of nature resulting from climate change and we have a growing concern about the scarcity of the resources we need to keep us and city life going – oil and energy, water and food. These issues fuel the fear of twenty-first century communities – that the apocalypse is nigh. Our children are less free and national health planners are telling us the young are getting fatter and less healthy.

The next generation can reshape the future. Our cities can be changed to encourage people to walk, to enjoy sunshine, to talk, to share and enjoy healthier lives. And they must be. More female architects and urban designers must be invited into the inner sanctum where our public places are designed. My work continues to teach me that women have a vital voice and role to play in community life and in making the places we need in our cities. Across the world in the past decade, architects and city planners have seized on the concept of the urban village as an idea that will help us to live using fewer resources; this is shorthand for more people living more closely together.

Despair and uncertainty about the future of the planet is with us. Governments are not as interested in city-making as they should be. It is left to civic leaders, their architects and planners and developers, who seek to build what communities want but without always being aware of what that is. Some governments are genuinely interested in the big picture of sustainability and in the health, culture, heritage, prosperity and quality of life, but simple economics still tends to get in the way of understanding what communities value. Becoming involved in making positive changes in our urban communities is not high on political agendas, with health, education, security and jobs coming first. These are important, but so is where and how people live. Governments need to invest in cities and the economics of strong, healthy communities and their contribution to real measurable community health, education and even jobs.

In Australia, organisations like Melbourne University's urban thinktank, the Grattan Institute, attempted to elevate the debate on these issues. The book summarising the issues as identified by Jane-Frances Kelly and Paul Donegan, *City Limits*, suggests that Australia's cities are broken and offers solutions to how we can fix them. Yet, while business and government work towards big solutions, it can be the small improvements in our streets and neighbourhoods that, piece by piece, strengthen our communities, enable people to connect and make life more enjoyable every day.

My decision to become involved to save Adelaide's colonial heritage, building on the groundwork of others, led to the introduction of local heritage listing in South Australia and the protection of the now much-treasured historic bluestone townscapes of North Adelaide and the city within the Adelaide Park Lands. It is said that timing is everything. Not belonging to a political party, I found support for this issue from people from all shades of politics, although it was a tough and bruising battle from those opposed to it.

I learnt that step changes in cities have a snowballing effect. Shady trees, fountains, bush, seating, markets, beautiful shop fronts, festivals, public art, and even the mass-planting of roses all create a daily life of surprise and greater comfort. When I was commissioned to write the village plans for the City of Sydney years later I brought this insight to them.

I still believe what I understood then, that preserving our stories and our heritage is protecting our culture. Developing for the future can work brilliantly only when we are able to hold onto the soul of the past and look to what is new. With a degree in history and English literature, not in town planning, I began a journey that has led me to work with communities and in cities across Australia to support the creation of more attractive, welcoming and useful places in our cities. Places can lift our spirits and be inclusive, and add surprise, excitement, wonder or some beauty to day-to-day life in the city. My local flower shop, the creation of Saskia Havekes, is a gift to everyone who passes its window, always alive with flowers. Much work still needs to be done to repair the outer suburbs of Australia's cities, where people deserve better than they have been given, and women have much to contribute to this.

I have met and worked with so many extraordinary women, women who have led change in the towns and cities of Australia through influence or leadership. I continue to work with many communities and have been privileged to work with some of Australia's and many of the world's great planners, architects, urbanists and inspired leaders in shaping exemplary places in many cities, bringing to the task my distinctively and proudly female sensibility. It was a chance to share their stories that led me to write *Places Women Make*. I have been fortunate to have wonderful feminist role models. My mentor and friend, Wendy McCarthy, and her friend, the first female Governor-General of Australia, Dame Quentin Bryce, and the first woman to be governor of an Australian state, Dame Roma Mitchell, have all been important influences on my community life and career, and for so many women who joined the workforce in the 1970s. Women like these inspire us all to act for a more equal Australia for women. Architecture is one of the last professional frontiers for women and our cities and communities need women's thinking, especially as architects, designers and catalysts for the special places women make.

In serving local communities Australian cities have historically been a battleground between state and local governments, each sometimes expressing 'not in my backyard' views. When people react strongly and indicate that some proposed change, whether from developers or governments, is unwelcome, they are usually justified in at least calling for a rethink. Rarely is the relationship between local communities, local councils, developers and governments an easy one. A genuine commitment to solving the problems in partnership is needed to make places successful. And good collaborative partnerships to ensure the good cities our children and their children deserve are also necessary. Communities and individuals should contribute to the plan – not only planners and developers – if we are to get the places we need. If we wait for governments to give us the cities we want, we may not get them. It has to come from people who care about their 'village'. And it must involve more women's thinking.

The battle for shaping our cities has high stakes. People resist change. It requires strength to stand between a developer and millions of dollars. It's almost fifty years since Joni Mitchell sang: 'they paved paradise, put up a parking lot', but the twenty-first century equivalent still occurs.

Australia's cities are still young. Each has its own sense of place and a personality that reaches back to the DNA of their founders. Australia's cities and suburbs are slowly becoming urban. Much work still needs to be done to repair the outer suburbs of cities. That will be the work of the next generation of urbanists. Changing our suburban centres will need skill, imagination, generosity, and especially the thinking of women, to create the urban 'living rooms' we now need.

The women whose stories have been recounted here have shaped Australian cities in many ways. All have been passionate, some as activists who believed that getting involved would improve our cities and our living, working and playing spaces. On the whole they have been well educated and fearless, natural communicators and happy to speak up when things seem off track. Rarely has their professional background been planning and architecture. It is just as likely to have been teaching, health, law or journalism. Their greatest qualities are common sense and tenacity, the capacity for communication and the possession of insight, compassion, humour and, most importantly, a female sensibility.

Cities matter. They are alive and they change, they are the places we live our lives and make our memories. It takes commitment, imagination and passion to make even the smallest idea for change blossom from an idea into a park, a playground, a library or a shaded street. With the influence of women, cities can be better places. Tomorrow's children need the places women make.

JANE JACOBS, *humanist and urbanist, a woman ahead of her time who believed cities needed the voice of women at the decision-making table because cities are for everyone and everybody matters.*

AFTERWORD

A TRIBUTE TO THE URBAN HEROINE JANE JACOBS

The urbanist Jane Jacobs understood that cities must be for everybody. That everybody matters. There has not been a voice like Jane Jacobs's in the public conversation about city-making since she wrote *The Death and Life of Great American Cities*. Published in 1961, it reflected on the postwar car-focused urban development of the 1950s. Jane Jacobs would have welcomed the return of the bicycle, the focus on walking and public transport and the take-up of her idea of big cities as a series of villages. The removal of cars from her city, at the heart of it in traffic-free Times Square, where people are regaining the city, surely would have thrilled her. The changes sweeping New York have inspired other big cities, like Sydney, to take up old ways as new ways to get around.

The biographies of Jane Jacobs describe her in a matter-of-fact way as an American–Canadian writer and activist with a primary interest in communities and urban planning. This could well be a description of many twentieth-century urban planners. Yet to architects and planners in the English-speaking world who have worked in shaping cities in the past fifty years, she is regarded as no ordinary activist. She is increasingly recognised as an oracle and the most significant woman urbanist of the last century. Her ideas influenced change for the better in many cities.

Born in 1916 in Scranton, Pennsylvania, and dying in Toronto, Canada, in 2006, Jane Jacobs witnessed during her adult life the transformation of North American cities.

Reading Jane Jacobs provoked my fascination with the idea that we can transform our cities into communities. I began a journey that has led me to work with communities across Australia to support making better places in our cities. Jane Jacobs's major work, published more than fifty years ago, was described by the *New York Times Book Review* as 'perhaps the most influential single work in the history of town planning' in the twentieth century, yet it is now not easy to find in bookshops or even libraries.

I hope in some small way this book reminds a new generation of the ideas of Jane Jacobs, who taught an earlier generation to care, to act, to get what we need in our streets, our cities and our everyday lives.

ACKNOWLEDGEMENTS

This book would never have been written without advice, encouragement and the many inspiring conversations with friends and family who believed it should be written. It is richer for the friends and colleagues who shared many stories of women they knew or told me their own stories or of places I should visit.

I especially thank Wendy McCarthy for teaching me, and so many women, we must tell our stories and for her friendship in challenging times. Susan Chenery kept me writing through the tough times and kept me laughing too. Andrea Nield so generously shared the world of architecture with a female perspective.

Without the loving support from my father Bob Jose, who has believed in my every passionate endeavour, always, I would not have taken the risks that led me to life as an urbanist in Sydney. I would not have these stories. I hugely thank my brother Nick Jose, for his patient questioning, guidance and love; and Claire Roberts for her unrelenting enthusiasm for the idea that urban heroines must be more central in Australia's cultural narrative. I thank Ken Maher for inviting me into the complex world of design and architecture; for support, inspiration and for sharing his world with me.

Charles Landry first suggested I write this book as a friend and global advisor on cities. He said: 'We need a book about city life now written by a woman.' I thank him for recognising women need more of a role in shaping cities and for his reading along the way. Huge thanks to Penelope Curtin, Dinah Dysart and Loredana Fyffe, the book's designer Liz Nicholson, and the publisher Michael Bollen, who loved the idea from the beginning and said write your story and perspective on city life. You have all helped me write *Places Women Make*.

THE WOMEN

My thanks go to the many women who have shared their stories with me and those whose stories I've retold:

Stephanie Alexander, AO
Brit Andresen
Elsa Atkin, AM
Sallyanne Atkinson, AO
Maria Atkinson, AM
Maybanke Anderson
Janet Angas
Robyn Archer, AO
Monica Barone
Barangaroo
Maggie Beer, AO
Professor Wendy Brady
Tessa Brady
Dame Beryl Beaurepaire
Battlers for Kelly's Bush
Lady Diamantina Roma Bowen
Hon. Carole Baker
Margaret Bailey
Sue Barnsley
Alison Beare
Hon, Dianne Beamer
Hon. Anna Bligh
Julieanne Boustead
Camilla Block
Rosemary Boucaut AM
Judith Brine, AO
Amanda Burden
Denise Scott Browne
Joan and Eileen Bradley
Susie Brennan
Kate Brennan
Cate Blanchett
Caroline Chisholm
Kerry Clare
Justine Clark
Louise Cox, AO
Michaelie Crawford

Julie Cracknell
Kate Cullity
Penny Collins
Olga Cohn
Elsie Cornish
Dame Sylvia Crowe
Mary Lou Jarvis
Francene Connor
Tanya Crothers
Lynda Dorrington
Delia Falconer
Elizabeth Farrelly
Kathryn Findlay
Suellen Fitzgerald
Fiona Foley
Lady Jane Franklin
Beatrix Jones-Farrand
Diane von Furstenberg
Neilma Gantner
Abbie Galvin
Isabella Stewart Gardner
Jackie Shannon Gillen
Vida Goldstein
Kathryn Gustafson
Bella da Costa Greene
Marion Mahony Griffin
Dame Zaha Hadid, DBE
Pat Hall
Wendy Harmer
Marcelle Hoff
Lady Ursula Hayward
Professor Sue Holliday, AO
Tara Hunt
Jane Irwin
Gertrude Jekyll
Betty James
Jane Jacobs

Acknowledgements

Maggie Jencks
Stephanie Johnston
Robyn Kemmis
Ulrike Klein
Louisa Lawson
Darani Lewers
Ann Lewis, AO
Margaret Lehmann
Hon. Susan Lenehan
Mary Lee
Louisa Lawson
Hon. Diana Laidlaw, AM
Janet Laurence
Wendy Lewin
Hon. Jane Lomax Smith
Dame Ruby Litchfield
Helen Lochhead
Anne Loxley
Dame Merlyn Myer
Patricia Michell
Elizabeth Macquarie
Hon. Clare Martin
Ruby Madigan
Anne Moran
Jude Munro, AO
Linda Mickleborough
Elizabeth Ann Macgregor, OBE
Helen McCabe
Winsome McCaughey, AO
Hon. Genia McCaffery
Elizabeth Macarthur
Joan Masterman
Emma Miller
Bette Midler
Teresa Moller
Yasuko Myer
Wendy McCarthy, AO
Hon. Lord Mayor Clover Moore
Dame Elisabeth Murdoch, AC, DBE
Roma Mitchell, AC, DBE, CVO, QC
Judith Nielson, AO
Juanita Nielsen
Rachel Neeson
Andrea Nield
Marianne North

Mary O'Kane
Jacqueline Kennedy Onassis
Lou Oppenheim
Alexis Ord
Margaret Olley, AC
Gaby Porter
Shelley Penn
Winnie Pelz
Hetti Perkins
Elizabeth Peck
Caroline Pidcock
Sunday Reed
Mary Reiby
Jesse Spinks Rooke
Imelda Roche, AO
Professor Dimity Reed, AM
Vita Sackville-West
Naomi Stead
Hon Lord Mayor Lisa Scaffidi
Caroline Simpson, AM
Emily Simpson
Margaret Simons
Gene Sherman, AO
Bridget Smyth
Lotte Smorgan
Goldie Sternberg
Lady Marigold Southey
Catherine Helen Spence
Barbara Schaffer
Martha Schwartz
Felicity Stewart
Anne Summers
Hannah Tribe
Kerstin Thompson
Jennifer Turpin
Ruth Park
Winnie Pelz
Christine C Quinn
Lucy Turnbull, AO
Edna Walling
Wendy Whiteley, AM
Jeanette Winterson
Janet Worth
Edith Wharton
Judith Wright

READING LIST

The information in *Places Women Make* comes from many sources.
Where I quote people I have not spoken with, their words are taken from documentary sources. The places I describe are real.

I read many books. I recommend them, for they tell a fuller story of many of the remarkable women about whom I have written.

Argent, Jill et al. 2010, *Carrick Hill: Heydays of the Haywards 1940–1970*. Friends of Carrick Hill, Wakefield Press, Adelaide.

Bianchi, Martha Dickinson (Ed.) 1924, *The Complete Poems of Emily Dickinson*, Little, Brown, Boston

Birmingham, John 2000, *Leviathan*. Random House: Sydney. New York.

Dixon, Trisha & Churchill, Jennie 1998, *The Vision of Edna Walling*. NLA: Canberra.

Flanagan, Richard 2012, *Wanting*. Random House: Sydney.

Harding, Lesley & Morgan, Kendrah 2010, *Sunday's Kitchen, Food and Living at Heide*. Miegunyah Press: Melbourne.

Heymann, C David 1989, *A Woman Named Jackie: An Intimate Biography of Jacqueline Bouvier Kennedy Onassis*. Lyle Stuart: New York.

Jong, Erica, 1973, *Fear of Flying*, Penguin Books

Kelly, Jane-Frances & Donegan, Paul 2015, *City Limits*. Melbourne University Press: Melbourne.

Ker Conway, Jill, 1989, *The Road from Coorain* An Australian Memoir, William Heinemann Ltd

Macquarie, Elizabeth 2011, *In Her Own Words: The Writings of Elizabeth Macquarie*. Published in association with Macquarie University: Sydney.

Magarey, Susan & Round, Kerrie 2007, *Roma the First – a Biography of Dame Roma Mitchell*. Wakefield Press: Adelaide.

MCA Almanac 2010, *The Gift of Ann Lewis, AO*. Sydney.

Mnookin, Sara James 2012, *Scatter My Ashes at Bergdorf Goodman*. Harper Collins: New York.

Moorhouse, Frank 2011, *Cold Light*. Random House: Sydney.

Park, Ruth 2000, *Ruth Park's Sydney*. Duffy and Snellgrove: Sydney.

Payne, Michelle 2011, *Marianne North: A Very Intrepid Painter*. Royal Botanic Gardens: Kew.

Pegrum, Roger 2008, *The Bush Capital: How Australia Chose Canberra as its Federal City*. Watermark Press: Boorowa, NSW.

Roberts, Jan, 1993, *Maybanke Anderson: Sex, suffrage and social reform*, Hale & Iremonger.

Stewart, Meg 2012, *Far From a Still Life: Margaret Olley*. Random House: Sydney.

Sumerling, Patricia 2012, *The Adelaide Park Lands: A social history*. Wakefield Press: Adelaide.

Tharp, Louise Hall, 1984, *Mrs Jack: A Biography of Isabella Stewart Gardener*. Little, Brown: Boston.

Van Zanten, David 2011, *Marion Mahony Reconsidered*. University of Chicago Press: Chicago.

PORTRAITS OF THE WOMEN

My thanks for the permission to use the portraits and photographs of the many women who shared their stories.

www.ingramcontent.com/pod-product-compliance
Lightning Source LLC
Chambersburg PA
CBHW071020280326
41935CB00011B/1433